"Deacon William Ditewig remains one of the most important voices writing on the diaconate today, and *The Deacon's Ministry of Charity and Justice* adds to his already remarkable body of work. Insightful, accessible and engaging, this new work should be required reading for anyone with a serious interest in the diaconate—from men in formation to deacons, pastors and bishops. Significantly, Deacon Ditewig's chapters on mercy and Pope Francis couldn't be more timely or valuable—reminding us of what we are called to be. Superb."

—Deacon Greg Kandra
Blogger and Journalist

# The Deacon's Ministry of Charity and Justice

*William T. Ditewig*

**LITURGICAL PRESS**
Collegeville, Minnesota

www.litpress.org

1     2     3     4     5     6     7     8     9

**Library of Congress Cataloging-in-Publication Data**

Ditewig, William T.
    The deacon's ministry of charity and justice / William T. Ditewig.
        pages    cm. — (The ministry of deacons)
    ISBN 978-0-8146-4824-7 — ISBN 978-0-8146-4849-0 (ebook)
    1. Deacons—Catholic Church.    2. Church work—Catholic Church.    I. Title.

BX1912.D3375    2015
262'.142—dc23                                                      2015021043

*For Mom and Dad,*

*Kathleen Powers Ditewig (1924–2014)*
*and William Frederick Ditewig (1917–86),*

*who were our first and best teachers in*
*Love, Faith, Mercy, Charity, and Justice*

# Contents

# INTRODUCTION

# Deacons and the *Diakonia* of the Church

In his document announcing a holy year of mercy, Pope Francis begins by referring to Christ as the "face of God's mercy" (*misericordiae vultus*). As we shall consider in more detail later, the deacon's ordination, configuring him in a particular way to Christ the Servant, places the deacon clearly into this image. Christ is the face of the mercy of God; Christ's deacons, therefore, might be said to be the hands of Christ, the hands of the very mercy of God. Nowhere is this participation more evident than in the deacon's participation in the church's own identity and mission as the people of God called to charity, justice, peace, and mercy.

In the Dogmatic Constitution on the Church (*Lumen Gentium*) the bishops of the Second Vatican Council opened their treatment of the diaconate with the words, "At a lower level of the hierarchy are deacons, upon whom hands are imposed 'not unto the priesthood, but unto a ministry of service.' For strengthened by sacramental grace, in communion with the bishop and his group of priests they serve in a diaconate [Latin original: *in diaconia*] of the liturgy, of the word, and of charity to the people of God."[1] Therefore, the first point to be made about the deacon's ministry is that it should always be seen through the single lens of service. There is, as consistently taught by the bishops of the United States in their various documents on the diaconate, "an inherent unity" between and among the deacon's ministry of Word, Sacrament, and Charity. This unity forms the theological and practical basis for all that follows.

1

In speaking of the ministry of the deacon, it must also be kept in mind that *diakonia* is not unique to the (ordained) deacon; all disciples are called to service. Furthermore, *diakonia* is not only the responsibility of the entire church: it reflects the very nature of the church. Second, as mentioned already, there is a frequently referenced "inherent unity" to that *diakonia*; its functions are not to be separated and they are to be fully integrated. Third, the diaconal nature of the church is not simply an *ad intra* concern affecting only the members of the church; there is an *ad extra* dimension: in the words of Pope Paul VI, "The Church has declared herself a servant of humanity."[2] In short, Catholic Christians have a vocation, a call from God, to respond to God's great and gratuitous love by living a moral life of service. We do what we do because of God's loving invitation to be one with God, and this covenant relationship is lived out through the way we in turn respond to others.

The goal of this introduction is to explore these three points in more detail in order to provide a backdrop for what is to come.

## I. *Diakonia*: The Threefold Ministry of Christ and the Nature of the Church

Just what are we to make of this word "diaconate" (Greek: *diakonia*; Latin: *diaconia*)? It is a term easily misunderstood. Often translated simply as "service," *diakonia* lacks a certain specificity of meaning. After all, just what *is* "service"? Many writers, in particular scholars such as John Collins, have pointed out that "service" is used in so many contexts it is hard to pin down: we receive "service" in restaurants, in automobile repair shops, in government offices. We conduct "services" in churches. Government officials and military personnel "serve" in various roles.

So it is not surprising to see people fall into a similar trap when considering the nature of the Order of Deacons within the context of *diakonia*. Not unreasonably, some simply equate deacons with *diakonia*: deacons are the ministers of the church who "do" *diakonia*. Furthermore, in this misunderstanding, *diakonia* is commonly thought to refer only to activities related to charity and justice. Before proceeding any further, then, we should consider more carefully *diakonia* within the tradition of the church.

An often-overlooked fact is simple grammar: the word *diakonia* is singular. There is *one* diaconate, one "service." This one diaconate, however, is expressed in the three functions traditionally associated with Christ's own ministry, sometimes referred to as "priest, prophet, and king" or "worship, word, and charity" or by the Latin *munus docendi*, *munus sanctificandi*, and *munus regendi* (the office of *teaching*, *sanctifying*, and *ruling*). As we shall see shortly, there is an "inherent unity" between these three functions.

The association of the deacon with the threefold ministry of Christ is an ancient one. Ignatius, the bishop-martyr of Antioch, is one of the earliest witnesses to this connection. His letters, written in the early second century, describe a clearly defined tripartite hierarchy of bishop with priests and deacons assisting. Ignatius compares the bishop to God the Father, presbyters to the College of the Apostles, and the deacons to Jesus Christ: "Correspondingly, everyone must show the deacons respect. They represent Jesus Christ, just as the bishop has the role of the Father, and the presbyters are like God's council and an apostolic band. You cannot have a Church without these."[3] "Let the deacons (my special favorites) be entrusted with the ministry of Jesus Christ who was with the Father from eternity and appeared at the end of the world."[4]

Ignatius is not the only writer to make this connection between Christ and the deacon. Polycarp, bishop of Smyrna, martyred about 156, writes to the Philippians, "It is necessary . . . to be subject to the presbyters and deacons as to God and Christ."[5] From Syria in the early years of the third century, the *Didascalia Apostolorum*[6] has this: "Let the deacon make known all things to the bishop, even as Christ to His Father. But let him order such things as he is able by himself, receiving power from the bishop, as the Lord did from His Father."[7] "The bishop sits for you in the place of God Almighty. But the deacon stands in place of Christ; and do you love him? . . . If then our Lord did thus, will you, O deacons, hesitate to do the like for them that are sick and infirm, you who are workmen of the truth, and bear the likeness of Christ?"[8]

Three points may be made: (1) All ministry, and in a particular way, ordained ministry, is grounded in and flows from the ministry of Christ; (2) the three functions of Word, Sacrament, and Charity have, therefore, a unity in Christ that cannot be compartmentalized or separated; and (3) the diaconate exercised by deacons is a participation in the larger *diakonia* of the church herself. It is important to remember that during the Second Vatican Council, when the bishops first write about *diakonia*, they are not speaking of deacons. Rather, that first reference is to the ministry of the bishops themselves. They write in *Lumen Gentium*,

> The bishops, in as much as they are the successors of the apostles, receive from the Lord, to whom all power is given in heaven and on earth, the mission of teaching all peoples, and of preaching the Gospel to every creature, so that all may attain salvation through faith, Baptism and the observance of the commandments. . . . For the carrying out of this mission Christ the Lord promised the holy Spirit to the apostles and sent him from heaven on the day of Pentecost, so that through his power they might be witnesses to him in the remotest parts of the earth, before nations and peoples and kings. . . . That office, however, which the Lord committed to the pastors of his people, truly is a service, which is called very expressively in sacred scripture a *diakonia* or ministry. (LG 24)[9]

Considering the traditional and ancient relationship of the deacon to the bishop, this citation carries significant ramifications for the role of the deacon. The deacon is ordained to assist and to extend the mission of the bishop himself. *Diakonia* is not simply the province of the deacon but of the bishop and the entire church; we deacons are simply privileged to participate in it in a particular way.

But here we must turn and ask a further question. The church has consistently taught about the unity of functions within the church's one *diakonia*. The bishops of the United States, for example, have stressed this point from the beginning of the renewed diaconate: "By ordination, the deacon, who sacramentalizes the Church's service, is to exercise the Church's *diakonia*. Therefore, 'the diaconal ministries, distinguished above, are not to be separated; the deacon is ordained for them all, and no one should be ordained who is not prepared to undertake each in some way.'"[10]

Why should this be the case, however? Why couldn't a person who simply will focus on charitable works be ordained? Or serve as a gifted preacher and teacher? Or concentrate on service as a sacramental minister? Why do we hold that the deacon must be competent in all three areas? Why couldn't the diaconate be "compartmentalized" so that some deacons could specialize in one or two areas rather than all three? The answer is quite simple: the unity of identity (who we are) and function (what we do) is found in Christ himself. Christ did not come simply to teach about the reign of God; he was, in himself, the

very initiation of that reign. Christ is the Word, and not simply the
teacher of the Word. Christ, in his kenotic self-giving, poured his whole
being into the concrete realities of human life in order to transform
and redeem us. There was no distinction in Christ between his Person
and his Mission. If deacons are to be true icons of Christ, then we must
try within our human limitations to have that same unity within
ourselves. This would seem to be sacramental significance of the deacon's ordination: the deacon is to incarnate this unity, to demonstrate
in his own ministry and life how all of these dimensions of discipleship
fit together. This is who the deacon is; what the deacon does specifically in service will flow from this sacramental identity.

## II. "Inherent Unity": The Perichoretic Diaconate

Let us consider the inherent unity of the threefold diaconate more
closely. I once spoke with a newly ordained deacon who was in the process of working on a "ministry agreement" with his new pastor. A "ministry agreement" is a form and process developed by a diocese in which
the deacon, his pastor or other ministerial supervisor (such as a chaplain
in a hospital, for example), the director of deacons, and the wife of the
deacon (if he is married) outline in some detail the specific ministries
in which the deacon will serve. During this process, they will consider
the three areas of Word, Sacrament, and Charity along with how much
time will be devoted to each in any given week or month. This can be
a very useful process, especially when there has been a change of pastor,
or the deacon is newly ordained, or there has been some significant
change in the life of the parish itself. Expectations can be clearly stated
and can be just as easily adapted as pastoral need dictates.

However, as this deacon pointed out, there was a problem at the
same time. He quickly realized that he had allowed his understanding
of ministry to become compartmentalized. He will do so much of *this*
ministry, then he will shift and do a certain number of hours in *that*
ministry, and then move on to the *next* ministry. He was rightly concerned that he might lose sight of how all of this was supposed to fit
together for the good of the church.

> The contemporary diaconate is grounded on the balanced exercise
> of the three-fold ministry; it is precisely in this balanced exercise
> that the deacon serves as a sacrament of unity, living through his

ministry and life, the marriage of witness to Christ, the praise of God and the care of neighbor. Christian discipleship demands *martyria, leitourgia* and *diakonia*: the deacon serves as a public and permanent sign of the unity binding these three dimensions together. His particular role is to remind the church of its own sacramentality, of its own *diakonia*, of the church's responsibility to be a "sign and instrument" and "leaven and soul" in creating a more just world.[11]

*Diakonia*, then, is a profoundly rich concept that transcends facile associations of the term with notions of menial service alone, or even less, "that ministry which deacons do"! It is here that an insight from the earliest centuries of our theological tradition might be helpful, namely, the concept of *perichoresis*.

As Christians began to spread the Good News of Christ, they had to come to grips with Christ's very identity. "Who do people say that I am?" was not just a question for the disciples assembled in Caesarea Philippi; it remains fundamental for all Christians. Flowing out of monotheistic Judaism, Christians struggled to describe the Christ. Was Jesus a human being called by God to be a prophet, teacher, and healer? Or was Jesus God who simply "acted" like a human being? Or was Christ (following Arius) a completely unique creature, neither truly human nor truly divine? After all, some mused, if they said that Jesus was God, then would that mean there were *two* Gods? For those earliest Jewish Christians, such a possibility was unthinkable: there was only one God. As the debate continued, various teachers tried to find a way to express what Christians believed about Christ and, therefore, about God. Eventually, the church was able to develop language that attempts to describe more clearly how all of these elements of faith might come together in a cohesive manner. Through the councils of Nicaea, Constantinople, Ephesus, and Chalcedon, language of *person, hypostatic union, nature, substance* were all used to describe Christ as well as the triune God. How do the two natures of Christ, human and divine, relate to each other in one Person? How are the three distinct divine Persons one God? While the classic schema reminds us that "the Father is not the Son, the Son is not the Spirit, the Spirit is not the Father," that same schema asserts that each of those Persons is God. The dynamic and inherent unity between and among those Persons began to be described by the Greek *perichoresis* (or its Latin translation *circumincessio*, circumincession). Oxford theologian Alister E. McGrath offers a good description of the term:

> This Greek term . . . came into general use in the sixth century. It refers to the manner in which the three persons of the Trinity relate to one another. The concept of *perichoresis* allows the individuality of the persons to be maintained, while insisting that each person shares in the life of the other two. An image often used to express this idea is that of "a community of being," in which each person, while maintaining its distinctive identity, penetrates the others and is penetrated by them.[12]

I propose that this term offers us a useful insight concerning the threefold *diakonia* of the church. While each area of service is unique, it penetrates the others and is penetrated by them. To preach and teach without the reality of our sacramental life and without the moral life in Christ would be nothing but empty rhetoric. To celebrate Sacrament without Word and Charity becomes little more than empty ritual. To focus on charity and justice without Word and Sacrament becomes social work that might be undertaken by any reasonable and caring person, and not the act of the disciple of Christ. What we want to remember is that each of the three areas of *diakonia* must constantly be understood and undertaken with an intentional relationship and interpenetration with the other two.

When preaching or teaching, how are we led to a more profound celebration of sacrament and worship as well as to a more active presence in caring for those at the margins of society or in any way in need? How does our celebration of sacrament flow from our breaking open the Word of God and how well does that help us go forth to serve others? How do we bring back our experiences from service "in the streets" to our growing understanding of God's Word and again lead us to celebrate an even richer sacramental life? In a very real, perichoretic sense, then, we cannot have one function without the others because each addresses, informs, and penetrates the others. This is the ministry of the church in which the deacon participates in a particular sacramental way. As Pope Paul VI observed at the end of the Second Vatican Council, "We stress that the teaching of the Council is channeled in one direction, the service of humankind, of every condition, in every weakness and need. The Church has declared herself a servant of humanity. . . . [T]he idea of service has been central."[13] This would become a consistent theme for Pope Paul, and it was echoed by John Paul II when he addressed US deacons in Detroit in 1988: "The service of the deacon is the Church's service sacramentalized. Yours is not just one ministry among others, but it is truly meant to be, as Paul VI described it, a 'driving force' for the Church's *diakonia*. You are meant to be living signs of the servanthood of Christ's Church."[14]

To further examine the threefold, integrated reality that is the church's own servant-identity, we turn to Pope Benedict's first encyclical, *Deus Caritas Est*, given to the church as a wonderful Christmas gift on December 25, 2005.

## III. The Fundamental Truth: God and God's Love for All

Pope Benedict begins with our most fundamental dogma, the nature of the triune God: "'God is love, and he who abides in love abides in God, and God abides in him' (1 Jn 4:16). These words from the First Letter of John express with remarkable clarity the heart of the Christian faith: the Christian image of God and the resulting image of mankind and its destiny. In the same verse, Saint John also offers a kind of summary of the Christian life: 'We have come to know and to believe in the love God has for us.'"

> We have come to believe in God's love: in these words the Christian can express the fundamental decision of his life. Being Christian is not the result of an ethical choice or a lofty idea, but the encounter with an event, a person, which gives life a new horizon and a decisive direction. . . . Jesus united into a single precept this commandment of love for God and the commandment of love for neighbor found in the Book of Leviticus: "You shall love your neighbor as yourself" (19:18; cf. Mk 12:29-31). Since God has first loved us (cf. 1 Jn 4:10), love is now no longer a mere "command"; it is the response to the gift of love with which God draws near to us. (*Deus Caritas Est* 1)

As Pope Benedict develops this thought further, he arrives at a very perichoretic description of the nature of the church through two "essential facts":

> a) The Church's deepest nature is expressed in her three-fold responsibility: of proclaiming the word of God (*kerygma-martyria*), celebrating the sacraments (*leitourgia*), and exercising the ministry of charity (*diakonia*). **These duties presuppose each other and are inseparable**. For the Church, charity is not a kind of welfare activity

which could equally well be left to others, but is a part of her nature, an indispensable expression of her very being.

b) The Church is God's family in the world. In this family no one ought to go without the necessities of life. Yet at the same time *caritas-agape* extends beyond the frontiers of the Church. The parable of the Good Samaritan remains as a standard which imposes universal love towards the needy whom we encounter "by chance" (cf. Lk 10:31), whoever they may be. (ibid. 25, emphasis added)

As we now turn our attention to the particular participation of the deacon in the church's ministry of charity and justice, it is hoped that the reader will bear in mind this fundamental and essential unity. This unity can serve as a constant reminder and prophetic challenge to all who serve in the person of Christ and in the name of the church. When all is said and done, how well do we connect the dots for the people we serve? How well do we live out the promise of the Word through the constant presence of God through our sacraments, and the concrete acts of charity, justice, and mercy as the graced moments of God's healing touch in the world today?

A final introductory comment is in order. The specific, concrete, and tailored responses of deacons to very unique pastoral needs will vary greatly from place to place, culture to culture, and diocese to diocese. This book could never serve as a kind of "directory of diaconal services" to be provided! Each deacon, along with his bishop and the priests, religious, and lay ministers of the diocese, must find his own creative responses to very specific needs within his own contexts. What I hope in this modest work is to suggest some foundational tools that might be considered in developing such diaconal pastoral strategies. In short, what means are available to the deacon to assist in carrying out his ministry? What follows, then, is a kind of deacon's "tool kit" for ministry.

# PART I

# Foundations for the Ministry of Charity

"Location, location, location" is a truism associated with realtors. Everything about the sale of a property depends upon where the property is located. In the "right" location, even a poor property might sell; in the "wrong" location, even a wonderful property will not. Location, they say, is everything. Where are we to "locate" the deacon's role in the ministry of charity, justice, and peace? How does this part of the deacon's ministry relate to the ministry of others, and how does it relate to the other dimensions of the deacon's ministry? Where do we situate the deacon?

In part 1 of this book, therefore, I want to address some foundational issues against which to consider the vocation of the deacon and his exercise of ministries of charity. Then, in part 2, we can dig deeper into practical issues and principles related to those ministries.

A stylistic note is necessary. As we shall soon encounter, the term "charity" (from the Latin *caritas*) has come to mean much more in the teaching and praxis of the church than simply giving someone what they need at a particular moment. Rather, we now explicitly link charity with justice, and in the more recent papal magisterium—especially with Pope Francis, but not exclusive to him—we have included mercy as well. While it will be more efficient at times to refer simply to "the ministry of charity," it should be borne in mind that, unless otherwise noted, the term includes all three notions of charity, justice, and mercy and the relationships among them.

# CHAPTER 1

# The Church as Sacrament of God's Mercy

## A Church of Servants

In order to understand the deacon's specific role and responsibilities for areas of charity and justice, it is necessary to peel back other layers of meaning, since no one serves within a vacuum. We begin by considering the nature of the church herself and, within this broader framework, introduce the role of the ordained within the church; we shall develop these themes in the subsequent chapters of the nature of vocation and on the specific characteristics of the diaconate.

The deacon, of course, serves in relationship with other deacons, with his bishop and the presbyters, with religious and laity. To consider his particular exercise of *diakonia* one must first consider the *diakonia* of the whole church to find how the deacon fits into the rich tapestry of ministry. We begin with the church: the people of God, the Mystical Body of Christ, and the temple of the Holy Spirit.

In particular we attend to Pope Paul VI's teaching that the nature of the church is diaconal; we are a servant church. As we saw in the introduction, Pope Paul stressed this fact at the end of the Second Vatican Council as he summarized its work: "We stress that the teaching of the Council is channeled in one direction, the service of humankind, of every condition, in every weakness and need. The Church has declared herself a servant of humanity. . . . [T]he idea of service has been central."[1] This character of the church is of critical importance when considering the role of the deacon. As Popes Paul and John Paul II frequently reminded us, deacons are to be the animators and promoters of the church's service, so the way in which deacons exercise their ministries involves more than the simple "doing" of service; rather, ordination confers a responsibility for leadership in service. This shall be examined in more detail in subsequent chapters, but for now we focus on the simple fact that the rationale for having deacons ordained for service can only be found within the servant nature of the church herself.[2] Deacons are not ordained simply to serve in lieu of others, or so that others do not have to serve. Deacons are ordained to serve in ways that will inspire, motivate, and lead others to join with them in service.

As this book was being prepared, Pope Francis released the Bull of Indiction to initiate the Extraordinary Jubilee of Mercy. Titled *Misericordiae Vultus*, the document begins with a simple and profound truth: "Jesus Christ is the face of the Father's mercy. These words might well sum up the mystery of the Christian faith."[3] Jesus, the Anointed of God, is (in the words of Edward Schillebeeckx) the "primordial sacrament," the preeminent pathway connecting humanity to the divine. When one encounters Christ, one encounters God. The church, therefore, as the people of God participates in this encounter through the power of the Spirit. Christ's mission becomes our mission, and in this instance, our mission is to be an expression of the Father's mercy to all. What has brought us to this point in our contemporary ecclesial self-understanding?

As has been well-documented, the Second Vatican Council took place after what Fr. John O'Malley (following Eric Hobsbawm) has referred to as "the long nineteenth century," and the political, social, industrial revolutions, world wars, the holocaust, worldwide economic collapse, and the global upheavals and devastation of the nineteenth and twentieth centuries.[4] It is also well-documented that the impetus behind many of the reforms of the council, and in a particular way the renewal of the diaconate, can be traced to the experiences of priest-prisoners in Nazi concentration camps during the Second World War.[5] The 2,700 bishops who assembled from around the world realized that the church had to examine itself closely and honestly in light of these developments, and that things had to change if the church was to be a more effective witness of Christ in the contemporary world. This point cannot be overemphasized: the world of the first half of the twentieth century was a profoundly violent and tragic place, and the

bishops who gathered for the council had all in various ways experienced war, economic depression, terrorism, totalitarianism, violence,
and a loss of confidence and meaning in human existence itself on
the part of many whom they served. Consider that outside St. Peter's
Basilica on October 11, 1962—the day the council opened—the inac-
curately titled "Cold War" was raging, atmospheric atomic testing was
taking place by the Soviet Union and the United States, and the following week would see the beginning of the Cuban Missile Crisis. At
the heart of all the pastoral needs of the world and the church was
the very nature of the church herself and how the church ought to
relate to the modern world. In short, who is the Catholic Church today?

Vatican II opens its teaching on the nature of the church by acknowledging this fundamental identity of the church herself as sacrament.
"Since the church, in Christ, is a sacrament—a sign and instrument,
that is, of communion with God and of the unity of the entire human
race—it here proposes, for the benefit of the faithful and of the entire
world, to describe more clearly, and in the tradition laid down by earlier
council, its own nature and universal mission" (LG 1). There are many
attempts to define a "sacrament," but the simplicity of the council's
words captures an essential element: a sacrament is both a sign (of
necessity, a *visible*, *outward*, and *public* reality) and an instrument, a tool
in the hands of God to bring about that which is signified.

Father Joseph A. Komonchak captured this mystery well when he
asked, "Who are the Church?"[6] Since the church *are* the people of God
and the Mystical Body of Christ and the temple of the Holy Spirit, then
each person of the church shares in this sacramental nature and mission. Each baptized person is a sign of unity; each baptized person is
to work as an instrument to bring about greater unity, a perfected
unity. This will be explored more deeply in the next chapter when we
discuss the nature of "vocation" in the church. For now, however,
starting with the idea that all the baptized share in this sacramental
identity and mission, how are we to understand the nature of mission
of the ordained within that ecclesial reality?

## Holy Orders for the Common Good

Within the church-as-Sacrament are celebrated the seven sacraments of the church: privileged ways in which people celebrate particular encounters with the divine. These sacraments are also signs

and instruments: they express an existing reality while at the same time challenging and deepening and perfecting that reality. Turning to the sacrament of orders, we refer to chapter 3 of *Lumen Gentium*. Paragraph 18 introduces this chapter on the hierarchical nature of the church, as the bishops explain the ministry of the ordained:

> In order to ensure that the people of God would have pastors and would enjoy continual growth, Christ the Lord set up in his church a variety of offices [ministries] whose aim is the good of the whole body. Ministers, invested with a sacred power, are at the service of their brothers and sisters, so that all who belong to the people of God and therefore enjoy true Christian dignity may attain to salvation through their free, combined and well-ordered efforts in pursuit of a common goal. (LG 18)

This common ministry of service that is shared by all the ordained is then particularized in the succeeding paragraphs, emphasizing the role of bishops from paragraphs 19–27, presbyters in paragraph 28, and deacons in paragraph 29, the final paragraph in the chapter. In 2005, the bishops of the United States promulgated, with a *recognitio* from the Holy See, the National Directory for the Formation, Ministry, and Life of Permanent Deacons in the United States. The context of the sacrament of holy orders within the overall sacramentality of the church, of those ordained to service within the whole body of believers, echoes conciliar teaching:

> Out of the body of initiated believers—anointed in the Holy Spirit through the Sacrament of Baptism, strengthened in the Sacrament of Confirmation, and nurtured with the Bread of Life—Christ calls some to ordained service. The Church, discerning their vocational charism, asks the bishop to ordain them to *diakonia*. [Author's note: the text here is referring to all who are ordained: bishops, deacons, presbyters; *diakonia* applies to all the ordained.]
> 
> "Holy Orders is the sacrament through which the mission entrusted by Christ to his apostles [and their successors] continues to be exercised in the Church until the end of time" [CCC, no. 1536]. Thus, it is the sacrament of apostolic ministry: "The mission of the Apostles, which the Lord Jesus continues to entrust to the Pastors of his people, is a true service, significantly referred to in Sacred Scripture as '*diakonia*,' namely, service or ministry" [Ibid., no. 22; cf.

LG, no. 24]. This *diakonia* "is exercised on different levels by those who from antiquity have been called bishops, priests and deacons." [LG, no. 28] (National Directory 23–24)

The diaconate participates, therefore, in the sacrament of apostolic ministry, exercised in its own unique way. "Exercised on different levels," the council says. On the level of the diaconate, then, it is fair to say that the diaconate is a "sign and instrument" (sacrament) of God's charity, justice, and mercy. It is a sign of something happening in the life of the church, but it also serves to bring something new. The people of God already serve each other and the rest of the world in countless ways: the diaconate is a sign of that existing service. On the other hand, much remains to be done to extend God's loving presence to those who remain in need: the diaconate is to be an instrument in finding new and creative ways to meet those needs. This has been a consistent and constitutive part of the deacon's ministry from the beginning. The *Didascalia Apostolorum* was composed in Syria during the early to middle years of the third century.[7] Probably no other ancient source is more descriptive of the relationship of bishop to deacon, of the source of the deacon's authority, of the deacon's responsibility to the poor, and even of the deacon's exercise of governance.

> Let the bishops and the deacons, then, be of one mind; and do you shepherd the people diligently with one accord. For you ought both to be one body, father and son; for you are in the likeness of the Lordship. And let the deacon make known all things to the bishop, even as Christ to His Father. But let him order such things as he is able by himself, receiving power from the bishop, as the Lord did from His Father. . . . But the weighty matters let the bishop judge. Yet let the deacon be the hearing of the bishop, and his mouth and his heart and his soul; for when you are both of one mind, through your agreement there will be peace in the Church.[8]

Deacons, through the sacramental grace received at ordination, become both signs and instruments—the hands—of God's mercy.

## Overview of the Deacon's Ecclesial Ministry

In the next chapter we will examine the deacon's ministry in greater detail and context, but for now we offer a brief introduction. In 1998, the Congregation for Catholic Education issued Basic Norms for the Formation of Permanent Deacons, including a particularly helpful, albeit lengthy, review of the deacon's identity and mission:

> The ministry of the deacon is characterized by the exercise of the three *munera* proper to the ordained ministry, according to the specific perspective of *diakonia*.
>
> *In reference to the munus docendi* the deacon is called to proclaim the Scriptures and instruct and exhort the people. This finds expression in the presentation of the Book of the Gospels, foreseen in the rite of ordination itself.
>
> *The munus sanctificandi* of the deacon is expressed in prayer, in the solemn administration of baptism, in the custody and distribution of the Eucharist, in assisting at and blessing marriages, in presiding at the rites of funeral and burial and in the administration of sacramentals. This brings out how the diaconal ministry has its point of departure and arrival in the Eucharist, and cannot be reduced to simple social service.
>
> Finally, the *munus regendi* is exercised in dedication to works of charity and assistance and in the direction of communities or sectors of church life, especially as regards charitable activities. This is the ministry most characteristic of the deacon.[9]

I would first draw attention to the opening sentence above: in referring to the three areas of ordained ministry, the Congregation concludes, "according to the specific perspective of *diakonia*." This emphasizes the essential point that there is one *diakonia*, expressed in three distinctive ways. The *munus docendi* (the "function of teaching") is often summarized as the ministry "of the Word"; the *munus sanctificandi* (the "function of sanctifying") is likewise summarized as the ministry "of Sacrament"; the *munus regendi* (the "ministry of ruling") as the ministry "of Charity and justice." However, all three of these distinctive functions are to be understood from the perspective of, and as a reflection of, a single worldview of *service*.

Consider as well the final observation from the citation above, that it is the *munus regendi*—dedicated to works of charity, assistance, and leadership—being "the ministry most characteristic of the deacon." This book focuses on this ministry of the deacon as a constitutive element of the nature of the church herself. Always flowing from the ministries of Word and Sacrament and leading back to them, and never apart from them, the deacon's exercise of charity, justice, mercy, and leadership extends the loving hand of God's constant love and mercy to all who are in need.

The bishops of Vatican II, after speaking of the sacramental grace received by the deacon during ordination, and suggesting various ways in which the deacon might carry out the responsibilities of *diakonia*, conclude by saying, "Dedicated to works of charity and functions of administration, deacons should recall the admonition of St Polycarp: 'Let them be merciful, and zealous, and let them walk according to the truth of the Lord, who became the servant of all'" (LG 29, referencing Matt 28:18ff.). With this understanding it is hoped that we can better appreciate the observation of the bishops of the Second Vatican Council when they referred to the functions of the deacon as being so difficult to experience in today's church and world and yet "so very necessary to the life of the Church" (ibid.). It was precisely this reasoning that led to their decision to seek the renewal of a diaconate permanently exercised in the contemporary church.

# CHAPTER 2

# God's Call and the Response of the People of God

### Introduction: The Primary Vocation of the Christian

One cannot speak of specific vocations in the church without first examining the nature of the vocation of the entire people of God. So, in this chapter we shall consider the vocation of the deacon from within the broader context of vocation itself. The meaning of any particular vocation within the church finds it proper meaning only insofar as it reflects the fundamental identity and vocation of the church. For example, for the church to have ordained ministers known as "servants" (*diakonoi*) finds its meaning only within a servant church. We frequently speak of our identity as a "priestly people" (1 Pet 2:9); however, we have ordained ministers known as "priests" as well: priests serving within a priestly church. Similarly, we have deacons serving within a diaconal church. So before turning to the specific nature of the deacon's role in the church's ministry of charity and justice, it will be helpful to briefly consider the foundation upon which that role—and, indeed, the entire diaconate—rests.

The church is all about relationships. In this chapter, then, we reflect on the nature of our relationship with God, and what the implications are for all of us—regardless of our state of life or role in the church—as we live our lives in response to God's call. For that's what all of this is ultimately about: our relationship with God and with each other. Vocation is nothing less than the moral life of the disciple, lived in response to God's gracious invitation.

## God's Call and Our Response

Call and response. From the beginning, the story of our relationship with God is one of call and response, of covenant between God and God's people. Recall *Lumen Gentium* 1, which we examined previously: "Since the church, in Christ, is a sacrament—a sign and instrument, that is, of communion with God and of the unity of the entire human race—it here proposes, for the benefit of the faithful and of the entire world, to describe more clearly, and in the tradition laid down by earlier council, its own nature and universal mission." That identification of church as the sign of an existing communion with both God and all of humanity is balanced with an understanding that this existing communion is far from perfect; the people of God are called to be instruments working for ever-greater communion. The church is not a finished product, and every member of the church shares in this responsibility to live this inner nature and universal mission. Since we are the church, we are those "signs and instruments" of covenant and communion. It has been this way from the beginning.

In the Hebrew Scriptures, the assembly of the people was referred to as *qahal Yahweh*. *Qahal* conveys a sense of a "called" people; it is derived from the word for "voice," and in this case it refers to a people called into existence by almighty God. Literally, we are speaking of a divine calling, often expressed by our English word "vocation," itself derived from the Latin *vocare*, to call. So often, however, when we use that word vocation in English we jump almost immediately to those ecclesial ways of life referred to as "religious life" or "ordained ministry." It is essential to recognize that there is a fundamental call to all human beings, a fundamental vocation that far precedes any subsequent and particular ecclesial vocation. All other vocations can only be properly understood in their relationship with this fundamental human vocation from God.

There is another point to make about that term *qahal*. During the preparation of the pre-Christian Greek translation of the Hebrew Scriptures known as the Septuagint, Jewish scholars had to find a Greek term to express the Hebrew *qahal*. The word chosen was ἐκκλησία (*ekklesia*), meaning literally "called out." The sense of a people called by God remains at the heart of the matter, and is the basis for all of our subsequent understandings of the "ecclesia" or church. We are first and foremost a people called into an assembly by God; we are the people of God precisely because of God's call, not our own choice. "You did not choose me but I chose you. And I appointed you to go and bear fruit, fruit that will last, so that the Father will give you whatever you ask him in my name" (John 15:16).

## Vocation as Bearing Fruit: The Moral Life of the Disciple

What more can be said about this covenant? It is a call, an invitation, to share in God's very life. In its landmark Dogmatic Constitution on Divine Revelation, the bishops of the Second Vatican Council put it this way:

> It pleased God, in his goodness and wisdom, to reveal himself and to make known the mystery of his will . . . , which was that people can draw near to the Father, through Christ, the Word made flesh, in the holy Spirit, and thus become *sharers in the divine nature*. . . . By this revelation, then, the invisible God . . . , from the fullness of his love, addresses men and women as his friends . . . , and lives among them . . . , in order to invite and receive them into his own company. (DV 2, emphasis added)

God's revelation is therefore God's loving invitation to share in God's own *divine nature*, made possible through the saving mediation of Jesus, the Christ of God. Deacons proclaim this invitation every time we place the drops of water into the wine at Mass and pray, "By the mystery of this water and wine / may we come to share in the divinity of Christ / who humbled himself to share in our humanity."

If we share in the divine nature, how do we now live our lives? Certainly, one who is living out a covenant relationship with God, who is breathing with the Spirit of God received during baptism, must live out that relationship accordingly. The opening paragraphs of the *Catechism of the Catholic Church*'s treatment of the moral life in Christ offer a succinct introduction to the life of a Christian disciple who has begun to "share in the divine nature":

> "Christian, recognize your dignity and, now that you share in God's own nature, do not return to your former base condition by sinning. Remember who is your head and of whose body you are a member. Never forget that you have been rescued from the power of darkness and brought into the light of the Kingdom of God." [St. Leo the Great,

Sermo 21 in nat. Dom., 3: PL 54, 192C.] . . . Coming to see in the faith their new dignity, Christians are called to lead henceforth a life "worthy of the gospel of Christ." [Phil 1:27.] They are made capable of doing so by the grace of Christ and the gifts of his Spirit, which they receive through the sacraments and through prayer. . . . Incorporated into *Christ* by Baptism, Christians are "dead to sin and alive to God in Christ Jesus" and so participate in the life of the Risen Lord. [Rom 6:11 and cf. 6:5; cf. Col 2:12.] Following Christ and united with him, [Cf. Jn 15:5.] Christians can strive to be "imitators of God as beloved children, and walk in love" [Eph 5:1-2.] by conforming their thoughts, words and actions to the "mind . . . which is yours in Christ Jesus," [Phil 2:5.] and by following his example. [Cf. Jn 13:12-16.][1]

The moral life of the Christian is more than simply following rules and laws; it is a way of life that is to be expected of one who has entered into the new life of sacramental initiation, into the life and relationships of the Trinity. God has invited; we have responded affirmatively to that invitation and now act accordingly. This is the relationship and the foundation upon which all further moral decisions are made, and the backdrop against which we come to understand the particular exercise of any particular ecclesial vocation, including diaconal ministry. We need to appreciate that all that we do flows from our sacramental initiation into divine life. God calls us to himself; our very life in Christ becomes our response in obedient faith, constant hope, and merciful love.

This is nothing alien to our human experience. When a couple are in love, when they give themselves totally, unreservedly, blissfully to each other forever, they want every subsequent act to reflect that love. That is perhaps why the Scriptures are so full of examples drawn from daily life, and especially the daily lives of those in love. When considering what one should do, the lover thinks first on whether the act is the kind of thing a person in love would or should do. Decisions are made and a way of life is undertaken that is formed not only by one's own moral compass about what is right for "me" but what is right for the "other" and for the shared relationship.

It is easy to see how this way of Christian life is the primary vocation of every disciple. This vocation is not merely a job or a profession that we undertake. Nor is it some part-time activity that is done as time and resources permit. Rather, the Christian vocation is truly a way of living and loving.

## The Moral Life: *Lex Orandi, Lex Credendi, Lex Vivendi*

Ever since the fifth century, we have accepted the insight of Prosper of Aquitaine that the way we pray (*lex orandi*) expresses and incarnates what we believe (*lex credendi*). Prosper's original statement was *"ut legem credendi lex statuat supplicandi"* ("that the norm of praying establishes the norm of believing"). Even before Prosper, this was already a common understanding in the Eastern traditions of the church. This insight stresses the fact that the symbolic discourse of the church's prayer and worship is the foundational expression of faith. Words alone are insufficient to express our belief. In more recent times, a third dimension is often added to this ancient axiom; namely, that praying and believing lead inexorably and constitutively to the *lex vivendi*, the norm of living. As Fr. Rick Hilgartner, former executive director of the USCCB's Secretariat for Divine Worship, wrote in an article for the 2009 Catechetical Sunday:

> In the early Church, it was the celebration of the liturgy and the Church's prayer that led to the development of articulated statements of faith – not the other way around. In light of that development, it is clear that sacraments celebrated well and experienced profoundly have the power to enlighten and to teach, to witness to what the Church professes and believes as we celebrate Christ and the power of his saving death and Resurrection in our lives. Those who prepare for and celebrate the liturgy, *lex orandi,* as well as those responsible for catechesis, *lex credendi,* need to trust that the sacraments can and will do so: that the living Word of God will inspire the faithful to more authentic Christian living, *lex vivendi.*[2]

Another way to view this might be to say: just as words alone cannot adequately express the faith we have received (and so we turn to sign and symbol in our sacramental life), so too words alone cannot adequately live out the faith we have received and the relationships that we have entered. We must walk the walk as well as talk the talk. How we live our lives also reflects our belief. It is so common to complain that the way some Christians act outside of Mass is often distinctly at odds with the way they act during Mass. *Lex orandi, lex credendi, lex vivendi* are all truly integral parts of the covenant life of the disciple.

So just what is "authentic Christian living"? Russell B. Connors offers an excellent summary of what it involves. The Christian moral life, he writes, "is nothing other than the recognition of the amazing gift of God's loving presence in our lives and our continuing effort to respond to that love."[3] He offers three points for consideration. First, it must be constantly remembered that "God is love." In other words, not only does God love us but the Judeo-Christian tradition has consistently maintained that God is love itself. God cannot be against his own nature; God is love and therefore God loves. Connors's second point is that God's love for us is unconditional: we have not earned it, we do not deserve it. God simply loves us, despite our faults and failings. Finally, God's love is transformative and effective. Connors puts it very well: "God's love is more than a feeling . . . it is a verb."[4]

I would suggest that three Scripture passages capture these elements very well and guide us further in our quest to understand what it might mean to live in response to God's love. Consider the First Letter of John:

> Beloved, let us love one another, because love is of God; everyone who loves is begotten by God and knows God. Whoever is without love does not know God, for God is love. In this way the love of God was revealed to us: God sent his only Son into the world so that we might have life through him. In this is love: not that we have loved God, but that he loved us and sent his Son as expiation for our sins. Beloved, if God so loved us, we also must love one another. No one has ever seen God. Yet, if we love one another, God remains in us, and his love is brought to perfection in us. (1 John 4:7-12, NABRE)

John tells us that God has loved us so much that he sent his only Son into the world; the famous hymn in the letter to the Philippians gives us a further insight into how Christ did that:

> If there is any encouragement in Christ, any solace in love, any participation in the Spirit, any compassion and mercy, complete my joy by being of the same mind, with the same love, united in heart, thinking one thing. Do nothing out of selfishness or out of vainglory; rather, humbly regard others as more important than yourselves, each looking out not for his own interests, but [also] everyone for those of others.
>
> Have among yourselves the same attitude that is also yours in Christ Jesus,

> Who, though he was in the form of God,
>     did not regard equality with God something to be grasped.
>     Rather, he emptied himself,
>     taking the form of a slave,
>     coming in human likeness;
>     and found human in appearance,
>     he humbled himself,
>     becoming obedient to death, even death on a cross.
> Because of this, God greatly exalted him
>     and bestowed on him the name
>     that is above every name,
>     that at the name of Jesus
>     every knee should bend,
>     of those in heaven and on earth and under the earth,
>     and every tongue confess that
>     Jesus Christ is Lord,
>     to the glory of God the Father. (Phil 2:1-11, NABRE)

Finally, the words of Christ himself, when summarizing the whole of the Torah:

> "Teacher, which commandment in the law is the greatest?" He said to him, "You shall love the Lord, your God, with all your heart, with all your soul, and with all your mind. This is the greatest and the first commandment. The second is like it: You shall love your neighbor as yourself. The whole law and the prophets depend on these two commandments." (Matt 22:36-40, NABRE)

In short, our moral lives—our vocations—begin when we respond to the simple truth that God has loved us to the point that Christ emptied himself so completely into human nature that he did not merely become human in some antiseptic or philosophical sense, but to the point that he became one with everyone, including and most especially the oppressed, the brutalized, the marginalized. Ultimately that is the message of the Cross ("even death upon a Cross"). Christ did not hold back from any aspect of human life. Consider: Christ could have emptied himself into our humanity, lived a "normal" life by being a tradesman like Joseph, getting married and having a family and living out a normal span of years. His life would have still been a model of how to live faithfully the covenant with almighty God. However, Christ did not do that. He immersed himself willingly into all of the messiness and cruelty of the time. Our God excludes nothing and no one from love and life. There is no aspect of human life that has not been graced by the presence of the divine gift. As the Philippians hymn reminds us, it is precisely because of this unconditional kenotic self-donation of Christ that our humanness is restored again to life in the Spirit. And the letter of John teaches us that because God has loved each of us so much, so too must we love one another. Christ's own message could not be clearer. When asked to summarize the Torah, he links the two tablets of Love of God and Love of Neighbor. We cannot claim to love one without the other. Why not? Because our triune God is not divided and since we are all in the image of God, we must also be united in love.

The *Catechism of the Catholic Church* is almost poetic: "The divine image is present in every [person]. It shines forth in the communion of persons, in the likeness of the unity of the divine persons among themselves" (1702). Furthermore, if we are in the image of God, and if we are immersed into that Divine Love in baptism and anointed by the Spirit as part of the Body of Christ, then we too must live as kenotically as did Christ. We too must pour ourselves out unconditionally for the good of others. The moral life of the Christian is not simply concerned with the acts of an individual human being (what might be called a "me-and-Jesus" approach to morality); it involves the acts of individual human beings in relationship with others. There are personal and social implications in every human act. It is only in this way, by recognizing both the personal and social dimensions of the Christian life, that we can truly follow Christ: first in his downward path of self-emptying for the sake of all and then in Christ's glorious return to the Father in restored, resurrected life.

## The Moral Life as a Life of Charity, Justice, and Mercy

We now probe more deeply into some specific aspects of this moral life, this Christian vocation. Pope Benedict's first encyclical, *Deus Caritas Est* (God Is Love), is a wonderful exposition of the role of charity in the life of the church, and this shall be our guide. Citing St. Augustine, "If you see charity, you see the Trinity," Pope Benedict writes,

> The Spirit is also the energy which transforms the heart of the ecclesial community, so that it becomes a witness before the world to the love of the Father, who wishes to make humanity a single family in his Son. The entire activity of the Church is an expression of a love that seeks the integral good of man: it seeks his evangelization

through Word and Sacrament, an undertaking that is often heroic in the way it is acted out in history; and it seeks to promote man in the various arenas of life and human activity. Love is therefore the service that the Church carries out in order to attend constantly to man's sufferings and his needs, including material needs. (19)

The encyclical's subsequent paragraphs have special significance for deacons. The pope teaches that love of our neighbor, while it is an individual responsibility of the disciple, "is also a responsibility for the entire ecclesial community at every level: from the local community to the particular Church and to the Church universal in its entirety. . . . Love thus needs to be organized if it is to be an ordered service to the community. The awareness of this responsibility has had a constitutive relevance in the Church from the beginning." Pope Benedict honed in on the "essential core" of our belief, that "within the community of believers there can never be room for a poverty that denies anyone what is needed for a dignified life" (ibid. 20).

> A decisive step in the difficult search for ways of putting this funda-
> mental ecclesial principle into practice is illustrated in the choice of
> the seven, which marked the origin of the diaconal office (cf. *Acts*
> 6:5-6). . . . Nor was this group to carry out a purely mechanical work
> of distribution: they were to be men "full of the Spirit and of wisdom"
> (cf. *Acts* 6:1-6). In other words, the social service which they were meant
> to provide was absolutely concrete, yet at the same time it was also a
> spiritual service; theirs was a truly spiritual office which carried out an
> essential responsibility of the Church, namely a well-ordered love of
> neighbor. With the formation of this group of seven, *"diaconia"*—the
> ministry of charity exercised in a communitarian, orderly way—became
> part of the fundamental structure of the Church. (ibid. 21)

Every disciple is to live a life of charity, justice, and mercy toward others. However, it is the pope's reminder that there is even more involved: that this is more than an individual or privatized response—as important as that is. The entire people of God—*as* the people of God—are also to live this fundamental and constitutive dimension of faith. We have now circled back to a point made above: every disciple is called to serve the needs of others, but all of these servants collectively form a church of servants working for the good of all.

# CHAPTER 3

# The Vocation of the Deacon and the Ministry of Charity and Justice

## The Origins of the Diaconate

In the words of Pope Benedict we find reference to the foundation and the origins of the diaconate in all of its forms. Deacons of every age are to incarnate this "fundamental ecclesial principle," this "essential core," this "constitutive" element of the church; namely, that Love, as expressed through charity, justice, and the mercy of God, must be more than the responsibility of each individual disciple. But it must also be ordered and organized within the very structures of the church herself. The church is servant; each disciple is called to be servant; and it is the deacons who are to assist with the ordering and structuring of the church's collective *diakonia*. As we shall see in part 2, Pope Francis is now challenging us further: to ensure that even the structures we have established within the church are functioning in a way that offers God's mercy through charity and justice.

From the earliest listing of the requirements for service as a deacon found in 1 Timothy, the deacon has been associated with the bishop in the care of the community, including caring for their physical needs. The legend of Deacon Lawrence of Rome from the third century captures critical ideas from the experience of the church: that the deacon is associated with the bishop and with the care of the church's temporal goods. This is why the magistrate picks Lawrence to collect the treasures of the church and not the bishop or one of the other deacons or subdeacons who had been arrested with him. And finally, when Law-rence brings all the poor of Rome to the magistrate, presenting them as the true treasure of the church, we find the deacon's association and responsibility for the care and concern for the poorest of the poor.

Even as the Order of Deacons gradually transitioned into a mere stepping stone to eventual ordination to the presbyterate, the associa-tion of the deacon for the organized care of the poor remained strong in many areas. Beginning around the fifth century, the care of the poor began to be handled by other ministers, including orders of religious women and men. Still we find exceptions. In Rome itself, for example, the emergence of the *diaconiae*, charitable distribution centers often staffed by deacons appointed by the pope, flourished in the seventh to ninth centuries. Architectural history paints a fascinating portrait. First, the distribution facility was quite basic, with a simple room in which goods could be stored and distributed. However, as the deacons spent more time there, they desired a specific place in which to gather for prayer, and a small "choir" area was added to the building where the deacons could chant the Divine Office. In existing examples, such as Santa Maria in Cosmedin, this area still contains the pulpit and the Easter candle. Finally, a sanctuary was added to the deacons' choir area so that Mass could be celebrated. What is fascinating is that, in the finished structure, the charitable distribution area has become both the place of charity and the nave of the church. The deacons' choir area links the nave with the sanctuary, with the ambo and the candle re-maining in that central area still the responsibility of the deacon. It raises an interesting question for reflection: Are the naves of our own parish churches today the place where we offer charity of all sorts to those most in need in our communities? There seem to have been as many as eighteen such *diaconiae* in Rome alone. The leadership of these centers, originally the responsibility of deacons appointed by the pope, gradually transitioned during this period to other clerics and laity.[1]

As I and others have noted elsewhere, the discussions to renew the diaconate as a permanent order of ministry emerged in Germany, France, and Italy during the nineteenth century. Briefly, there were three general concerns raised in those early days of the renewal. First, there was concern that the existing gap being experienced in many areas between official church structures and officials and ordinary people was broad and deep. It was thought that deacons could help bridge that gap. Second, many of the Protestant churches were beginning to organize, especially in Germany, in support of charitable activities. Many of these Protestant churches were reinstating deacons precisely to coordinate their charitable outreach (although their theological understanding of the diaconate was significantly different from a Catholic point of view). Nonetheless, Catholics were looking for their own way to do the same thing: how might they better organize themselves to support such activities. Third, also in the relationship between Catholic and Protestant churches, it was realized that deacons had a strong biblical and patristic presence and that as such they were needed to complete the traditional triad (at least since Ignatius of Antioch) of deacon, presbyter, and bishop. Notice the practical bent to all of these concerns. As Pope Benedict wrote, "Love needs to be organized. . . ." Rather sketchy notions of a renewed diaconate appeared sporadically throughout the nineteenth century.

In the first third of the twentieth century, however, there was little time for theological speculation on the possible return of a diaconate permanently exercised in the Latin church. Instead, people around the world were dealing with violence, death, and destruction on a scale never before experienced. Survival became the highest priority. Two world wars, regional unrest, worldwide economic collapse, and the rise of Communism, Fascism, and Nazism transformed Europe and, eventually, the world. After Adolf Hitler came to power in 1933 in Germany, especially after many private institutions and structures were taken over by the Third Reich, some church leaders opined that perhaps the heads of Catholic charitable institutions (such as Caritas) might be ordained. In that way, although they would still be at personal risk, they themselves would be part of the official structure of the church and retain some measure of autonomy, however fragile.

It would be in Dachau concentration camp that the notion of a contemporary "permanent" diaconate was born in the discussions of hundreds of priest-prisoners incarcerated there. Two ideas surface in their conversations. First, they were overwhelmed by the general ineffectiveness of religion in general and the Catholic Church in particular in helping to prevent or at least ameliorate those tragedies. Were there ways in the future to become more effective in dealing with the world and the conditions leading up to such horrific consequences? In the camp, many ideas of reform and renewal came to light and, following the war, these priest-survivors began to share these ideas in articles, in books, and through their own pastoral ministries. One of the ideas, which had been kicking around for almost one hundred years, was that of a renewed diaconate. Now there seemed a particular relevance and urgency for such a diaconate. Not because of any shortage of priests, but out of a desire to have the world reminded of the Servant Christ as well as Christ the High Priest. If the church could be seen as the face of Christ the Servant, perhaps the church could reach places she had not been able to go before. We see this idea expressed beautifully years later by one of those council fathers who voted for the renewed diaconate, Pope John Paul II. During a catechesis on the diaconate, he observed, "A deeply felt need in the decision to re-establish the permanent diaconate was and is that of greater and more direct presence of Church ministers in the various spheres of the family, work, school, etc., in addition to existing pastoral structures."[2] Joseph A. Komonchak, in his own extensive work on the Second Vatican Council, once observed that "the renewal of the diaconate was not accomplished because of a shortage of priests but because of a shortage of deacons."

Another idea behind the renewal of the diaconate, as outlined by the survivors of Dachau, was that the diaconate would be part of a much larger program of church reform and renewal. It was quite obvious to everyone that the world could not continue with the *status quo*. Before the end of the Second World War, the atomic age dawned with the dropping of atomic weapons on Hiroshima and Nagasaki, and then the beginning of the so-called "Cold" War. No, things could clearly not continue as they were. Millions of people had already died violently in the first half of the twentieth century, and if matters did not change drastically, humanity now had the power to destroy itself and the planet. It is still not unusual to hear some contemporary observers opine that previous church councils had convened during times of crisis, but—in this point of view—there was no crisis facing the church in the postwar years. To them, especially in the United States, they saw full seminaries and convents, creation of new parishes and schools, and a kind of 1950s "golden age" for Catholicism. Therefore, again in this view, there should have been no need for Vatican II. It must be said, however, that this "isolationist" point of view did not reflect global reality at all, and certainly not the point of view of the survivors of the Second World War, including those priest-survivors of concentration camps such as Dachau. Given the political and military situation alone in the world, few greater crises had ever faced the church and the world.

Therefore, less than twenty years after the end of the war, St. John XXIII launched the entire church on a global program of reform and renewal, focused on the nature of the church herself and her role in the contemporary world, as the bishops of the world gathered to inaugurate the Second Vatican Council. Pope John called the bishops to a new and daring approach to contemporary life and ministry, perhaps best expressed in his famous opening address on October 11, 1962. He spoke of the balance between the "sacred deposit of Christian doctrine" and its relationship to the changing demands of the contemporary world:

> In order, however, that this doctrine may influence the numerous fields of human activity, with reference to individuals, to families, and to social life, it is necessary first of all that the Church should never depart from the sacred patrimony of truth received from the Fathers. But at the same time she must ever look to the present, to the new conditions and new forms of life introduced into the modern world, which have opened new avenues to the Catholic apostolate. . . . The substance of the ancient doctrine of the deposit of faith is one thing, and the way in which it is presented is another.[3]

## What Is Needed Most: *Novus Habitus Mentis*

This task of constant translation of ancient truths into contemporary sociocultural language demands a constant effort, a new way of approaching pastoral problems. Pope Paul VI began to refer to this frequently as a *novus habitus mentis*, a new way of thinking. During the final days of the council, he first used this expression on Saturday, November 20, 1965, when he addressed the commission revising the Code of Canon Law. While he used the expression initially in reference to the way the revised Code of Canon Law would need to be approached in light of the council, its effect is much broader. The revised Code would have to mirror, enable, and empower the servant church as described by Vatican II. "Now, however, with changing conditions . . . canon law must be prudently reformed; specifically, it must be accommodated to a *new way of thinking proper to the second ecumenical council of the Vatican, in which pastoral care and new needs of the people of God are met*" (emphasis added).[4] What is striking even at first reading is that this "new way of thinking" is to be no mere cognitive process. Nor is it simply a legal principle. Rather, this "new habit of mind" has the practical end of concrete pastoral care and meeting the needs of God's people. As we move forward to consider the deacon's role in the church's ministry of charity, justice, and mercy, this shall be the sacramental expression of *novus habitus mentis*: making sure that everything deacons do is focused on meeting the very real and messy needs faced by people every day. There is nothing theoretical or hypothetical about it: the standard of measurement is precisely how well these needs are actually met. Pope Francis expressed this new attitude well in *Evangelii Gaudium*:

> There are ecclesial structures which can hamper efforts at evangelization, yet even good structures are only helpful when there is a life constantly driving, sustaining and assessing them. Without new life and an authentic evangelical spirit, without the Church's "fidelity to her own calling," any new structure will soon prove ineffective.
>
> I dream of a "missionary option," that is, a missionary impulse capable of transforming everything, so that the Church's customs, ways of doing things, times and schedules, language and structures can be suitably channeled for the evangelization of today's world rather than for her self-preservation. The renewal of structures demanded by pastoral conversion can only be understood in this light: as part of an effort to make them more mission-oriented, to make ordinary pastoral activity on every level more inclusive and open, to inspire in pastoral workers a constant desire to go forth and in this way to elicit a positive response from all those whom Jesus summons to friendship with himself. As John Paul II once said to the Bishops of Oceania: "All renewal in the Church must have mission as its goal if it is not to fall prey to a kind of ecclesial introversion."[5]

Father Ladislas Orsy has written that *novus habitus mentis* may be rendered in a variety of ways: most literally as "new habit of mind," "new habit of the mind," or even "a mind with a new disposition," "a new mentality," or "a new mind." "The point is that the pope asked for a change in the mind itself."[6] Orsy, building on Bernard Lonergan, goes even further when he writes that "to acquire a new disposition of the mind means to enter into a new field of vision; that is, into a new horizon."[7] As we have already seen, Pope Paul himself framed that new horizon when he characterized the entire work of the council as that of identifying the church as the servant of humanity. Again we find Pope Francis reflecting this new horizon:

> Pastoral ministry in a missionary key seeks to abandon the compla-
> cent attitude that says: "We have always done it this way." I invite
> everyone to be bold and creative in this task of rethinking the goals,
> structures, style and methods of evangelization in their respective
> communities. A proposal of goals without an adequate communal
> search for the means of achieving them will inevitably prove illusory.
> I encourage everyone to apply the guidelines found in this document
> generously and courageously, without inhibitions or fear. The impor-
> tant thing is to not walk alone, but to rely on each other as brothers
> and sisters, and especially under the leadership of the bishops, in a
> wise and realistic pastoral discernment. (*Evangelii Gaudium* 33)

The diaconate is a wonderful example of how the kind of transformation being suggested by Pope Francis can happen. Renewing a contemporary diaconate was truly reflective of seeing things in a new and
challenging way. Consider for a moment that none of the council fathers
at Vatican II had ever known or experienced a "permanent" deacon.
They had no pastoral experience upon which to build such a diaconate,
and they had no idea what problems might take place or how such an
idea might realistically be implemented. As I have sometimes asked
my students, "What kind of reaction would you get at a meeting if you
suggest doing something that has not been done before, or at least not
done in the lifetime of anyone at the meeting?" The answer is that
many people would look at you as if you were crazy. And yet that is
precisely what the bishops at Vatican II voted overwhelmingly to do.
Although there had been exceptions to the norm over the centuries,
there had not been a "permanent" diaconate in well over a millennium.
The council fathers deemed it necessary for the contemporary church,
however, that deacons return to the stage of ministry, an idea literally
born behind bars during World War II. As a reflection of this "new way
of thinking," the vision behind the renewal of the diaconate was simple:
to work to create a world in which the tragedies and horrors of the
twentieth century would not be repeated. That's why the diaconate
was revivified by the council: nothing more and nothing less.

## Conclusion

The deacon's ministry can now be seen in proper perspective, a
perspective that goes to the very heart of our identity as members of

God's people, called to share in God's very nature through the kenotic love of Christ and the transforming power of the Spirit. As members of this people, each of us is called (vocation) to live out the expectations of discipleship (the moral life): to love God and our neighbors in the same way that God has already loved us. Within the members of this people, some are called by God through the ministry of the church to serve the rest in particular ways. For those ministers known as deacons, this means that they serve in a way that stirs up, enflames, and empowers the rest of the church to serve others in their turn. Deacons therefore serve, as all the baptized are called to do; but they are also called and empowered by sacramental grace to lead. Ordination, as Nathan Mitchell and others have long pointed out, confers a leadership role tailored to each of the three orders of bishops, deacons, and presbyters. The deacon's participation in the one priesthood of Christ is unique among both the baptized and the ordained:

> By restoring the diaconate as a permanent role with the church's ordained leadership, Paul VI implicitly broke the long-standing connection between ordination and "sacramental power.". . . Theirs is a ministry, rooted like all others in a recognition of baptismal charism, that places pastoral leadership before sacramental power. The diaconate represents, then, those New Testament qualities of ministry which Schillebeeckx has aptly described as "the apostolic building up of the community through preaching, admonition and leadership." The restoration of the diaconate is thus important not because it resurrects an ancient order that had all but faded in the West, but because it affirms the principle that *recognition of pastoral leadership is the fundamental basis for calling a Christian to ordained ministry.*[8]

In the next chapter we will examine more closely this particular type of servant-leadership that is exercised by the deacon in a most focused way through his participation in the ministry of charity, justice, and mercy.

# CHAPTER 4

## The Deacon as Apostolic Leader in *Diakonia*

### Introduction: Leadership and the Deacon

Nathan Mitchell's observation about the significance of the diaconate's renewal lying in the recognition of pastoral leadership will serve as the lens through which we will develop an understanding of the deacon's role in the ministry of charity and justice.[1] It is important for us to consider how the deacon is called to lead. The title of this chapter is taken from the National Directory for the Formation, Ministry, and Life of Permanent Deacons in the United States, promulgated by the episcopal conference of the United States in 2005. The leadership responsibility of the deacon is clearly identified as being not only a witness to charity and justice but a guide for others to follow as well. As part of the holy year of mercy called by Pope Francis, deacons will have their own jubilee day, and the commentary that accompanied the publication of the official calendar for the holy year included the statement, "Another event will be for deacons who by their vocation and ministry are called to preside in works of charity in the life of the Christian community."[2] As we shall see, the magisterial literature on the diaconate, especially vis-à-vis the church's ministry of charity and justice, highlights the deacon's leadership. The deacon is charged with "presiding in works of charity."

Much of the official literature on the renewal of the diaconate includes considerable references to the deacon's leadership roles. Even within secular literature, much has been written over the years about "servant-leadership," yet that term's application to the ministry of the deacon has not always been fully appreciated. For example, I once had a deacon approach me after a talk about diaconal leadership with the observation, "I'm a servant, not a leader." On a different occasion, during a training session on deacon formation, the facilitator (not a deacon) made the comment, "Good deacons are lousy leaders, and good leaders are lousy deacons." I was particularly troubled by this comment, since in the next room were hundreds of people, most of them deacons, who were serving in diocesan leadership positions. The facilitator's comment made a bizarre indictment about that group: either each bishop had chosen poor leaders for his staff (but good deacons), or he had good leaders on the staff but poor deacons. Comments like these influenced me to study the nature of diaconal leadership: Were the concepts of "deacon" and "leadership" truly incompatible? Eventually I would write and defend a doctoral dissertation titled "The Exercise of Governance by Deacons: A Theological and Canonical Study." I have written extensively about this issue, so there is no need to rehearse the material here. On the other hand, I hope that the reader will find some time to review those earlier presentations, as they form the foundation for the treatment here. The bottom line is this: leadership and governance are not alien to the diaconate; in fact, true servant-leadership has been a hallmark of the deacon from the very beginning. We will examine how much of this is treated within the Code of Canon Law in order that we may realize how this leadership language found in magisterial documents has found legal expression in the Code. It can also help us realize just what options already exist in the law for deacons and, in our particular quest, for deacons in their exercise of a ministry of charity and justice.

Ecclesial leadership by deacons is obvious already in the references to the diaconate in the New Testament and in even more explicit ways throughout the "golden age" of the ancient diaconate as found in the patristic sources. Even during the time of the order's transformation into a transitional step to the presbyterate, exceptions existed. We have the examples of deacon-leaders, including Francis of Assisi, English Cardinal Reginald Pole (who presided as papal legate over the first session of the Council of Trent in the sixteenth century), and Cardinal Giacomo Antonelli (Pius IX's Secretary of State) and Cardinal Teodolfo Mertel (head of Roman Rota)—both deacons serving in the nineteenth century. And we must not forget those dozens of Roman deacons who were elected to serve as Bishop of Rome upon the death of their immediate predecessors.

It is a fascinating history, but our focus is on the contemporary renewal of the order. Today, deacons emerge in the magisterial literature as apostolic leaders in *diakonia* and this will influence all of the deacon's ministries, and especially the ministry of charity and justice.

## Leadership and Governance

The first clue that deacons are to exercise leadership is found in *Lumen Gentium* 29 itself. The bishops include a significant phrase in this section, yet it is a phrase sometimes omitted in English translations. The bishops write that it will be the responsibility of the various episcopal conferences, with the approval of the pope, to decide "whether and where it is opportune for such deacons to be appointed for the care of souls [*utrum et ubinam pro cura animarum huiusmodi diaconos institui opportunum sit*]." Father John Beal has noted that *cura animarum* is "a phrase with historic associations with the power of jurisdiction."[3] We have suddenly found ourselves, with that one phrase, entering into the realm of canon law concerning the concept of ecclesial governance.

This is an extremely complex area, and it is beyond the scope of this project to examine it in any great detail. Nonetheless, it must be considered to some degree, since it is part of the deacon's "tool kit." It's important that deacons and those with whom they serve are aware of the authority and the options given to the deacon by the universal canon law of the church. For those who may wish to explore the notion of governance by deacons in more detail, I refer them to the dissertation referenced above.[4] For now, however, it is important to distinguish our terms from the outset, especially leadership and governance.

Governance is a subset of leadership. All governance is an exercise of leadership; not all leadership, however, is a function of governance. Juridically, governance conveys positional authority over a portion of the people of God; it does not necessarily speak to the quality of leadership to be exercised in that position. Full governance is enjoyed only by a diocesan bishop, in that he has "full, proper, and immediate" jurisdiction over the particular church (diocese) entrusted to him. Presbyters and deacons, each in their own way, participate to a lesser degree in this exercise of governance. Presbyters share in the sacerdotal order of the bishop, and thereby may assume offices involving the full care of souls, but always under the supervision and direction of the bishop. Presbyters are further constrained from full governing authority since they have no immediate authority over the sacrament of orders: they do not ordain others into ministry. Deacons share in the diaconal order of the bishop, thereby assuming offices involving the care of souls to the extent permitted by diaconal ordination and ecclesiastical faculties.

Leadership describes how governance is to be exercised, and provides the spiritual connection between those in authority and those they serve. Leadership is more than simple management of resources; leadership is the intangible quality of care, concern, and sacrifice for others that is found in all successful and effective leaders in any field. In sum, attempting to describe the exercise of governance without a commensurate appreciation of the nature and qualities of the more theological concept of servant-leadership would be inadequate and insufficient to the discussion of any order of ministry in the church, including that of the deacon.

John Beal continues: "The 'care of souls' refers to the pastoral activity of the Church to teach, sanctify, and govern the people of God. . . . [T]he 'care' of souls is the official activity whereby authorized persons provide ministry to people with a view to their salvation."[5] It is possible to distinguish different levels of *cura animarum*. Canon 150, for example, refers to the *full* care of souls, in which case, the office must be filled by a priest (presbyter or bishop). Other canons refer to persons other than priests who share to some degree in the care of souls. Father James Provost identifies, for example, coadjutor and auxiliary bishops, parochial vicars, "deacons and lay persons involved in the care of souls [c. 517 §2], some chaplains."[6] Simply put, the care of souls is a responsibility of the diocesan bishop, a responsibility that attaches to a particular office or ministry (such as that of pastor) to ensure that it is carried out, a responsibility that involves all three areas of teaching, sanctifying, and ruling. Furthermore it is helpful to remember that from the earliest historical sources through contemporary documents on the diaconate, deacons have been described as "dedicated to works of charity *and functions of administration*" (LG 29, emphasis added). Functions of administration, as shall be seen, frequently fall into the category of administrative governance, although they never constitute the capacity for *full* care of souls. With these considerations, then, what functions of governance are extended to deacons under the code?

Canon 483 §2 (c. 253 in the Eastern code) permits deacons, as clerics, to serve as diocesan chancellors and notaries. Similarly, c. 512 §1 (c. 273 in the Eastern code) refers to clerics being part of a bishop's diocesan pastoral council; while deacons are not mentioned explicitly, neither are they excluded. Unless particular law (in this case, law decreed by the diocesan bishop) restricts membership of a diocesan pastoral council to the laity, deacons may serve in this capacity. Canon 536 §1 (c. 295 in the Eastern code) addresses the establishment of parish pastoral councils; the pastor is to preside, while "those who share in pastoral care by virtue of their office in the parish" are involved in the council in order to "assist in fostering pastoral activity" (*ad actionem pastoralem fovendam suum adiutorium praestent*). This would include clerics (obviously including deacons) assigned to the parish by their bishop. Canons 1421, 1428 §2, and 1435 (paralleled by cc. 1087, 1093, and 1099 in the Eastern code) permit deacons, as clerics, to serve when qualified as judges and various court officials.

The deacon's ministry, however, goes deeper than simply enumerating specific canons with regard to governance. Let us probe a bit deeper into the teachings surrounding the revision of the Code and the renewal of the diaconate.

The documents of Vatican II (in particular, *Lumen Gentium*), other canons, and the liturgical books themselves identify particular diaconal functions. According to *Lumen Gentium* 29, for example, the deacon is to administer baptism solemnly, care for the Eucharist and give Holy Communion, assist at and bless marriages in the name of the church, carry Viaticum to the dying, read the Scriptures to the people and exhort and instruct them, preside over worship and prayer, administer sacramentals, and officiate at funeral and burial rites.

Paul VI's 1967 *motu proprio*, *Sacrum Diaconatus Ordinem*, provided the norms for the renewal of the diaconate. The pope expanded the duties described in LG 29, resulting in eleven sets of diaconal functions:

1. To carry out, with bishop and priest, all the roles in liturgical rites that the ritual books attribute to him
2. To administer baptism solemnly and to supply the ceremonies that have been omitted at baptism in the case of an infant or adult

3. To have custody of the Eucharist, to distribute it to himself and to others, and to impart Benediction of the Blessed Sacrament to the people with the pyx

4. To assist at and bless marriages in the name of the church when there is no priest present, with delegation from the bishop or the pastor, so long as everything else commanded in the Code of Canon Law is observed, and with no infringement on Canon 1098, in which case what is said of a priest is to be understood of a deacon as well

5. To administer sacramentals, and to preside at funeral and burial rites

6. To read the Scriptures to the faithful and to teach and preach to the people

7. To preside over the offices of religious worship and prayer services when there is no priest present

8. To direct Bible services when there is no priest present

9. To do charitable, administrative, and welfare work in the name of the hierarchy

10. To legitimately guide outlying communities of Christians in the name of the pastor and the bishop

11. To foster and aid the lay apostolate[7]

Nearly all of these functions involve servant-leadership: the deacon is said to "preside, direct, guide, foster, aid, teach, preach, administer." Several of these functions are directly related to areas traditionally associated with acts of governance:

> To preside over the offices of religious worship and prayer services when there is no priest present

> To do charitable, administrative, and welfare work in the name of the hierarchy

> To legitimately guide outlying communities of Christians in the name of the pastor and the bishop

The context for all of this returns us to Vatican II. Bertram F. Griffin, among others, has demonstrated the centrality of the threefold *munus* of Christ within the documents of Vatican II. "The doctrine of the three-fold *munera*, originally a Christology, was translated into an ecclesiology by the Second Vatican Council, and many of the documents of the Council are structured in terms of these three offices or ministries."[8]

We are concentrating on the third of these three *munera*, the *munus regendi*. Vatican II describes the *munus regendi* in terms that go far beyond an exercise of governance; indeed, *munus regendi* can be said to extend "even to the transformation of the temporal order, and the Church's commitment to spiritual and corporal works of mercy."[9] This fact will be significant later as we treat the importance of the works of mercy in the ministry of the deacon. Finally, the *munus regendi* includes "the administration of temporalities for the sake of worship, ministry and the care of the poor."[10] Since these areas are covered in different sections of canon law, the deacon and his bishop must attend to the whole of the Code to find all the possibilities for ministry reflected there. In short, the ministry of leadership and governance in which the deacon participates in virtue of his ordination is a broad-based reality that cuts across the entire spectrum of the triple *munus* of teaching, sanctifying, and ruling.

The deacon, of course, is a member of the clergy, and the law spells out certain aspects in that regard which affect our examination. Canon 207 §1 situates the clergy among the Christian faithful: "By divine institution, there are among the Christian faithful [*inter christifideles*] in the Church sacred ministers who in law are also called clerics; the other members of the Christian faithful are called lay persons." Canon 1009 §1 identifies these clerics as members of the episcopacy, the presbyterate, and the diaconate. Canons 1008 and 1009 §3 of the revised Code expand the description of clerics:

> By divine institution, some of the Christian faithful are marked with an indelible character and constituted as sacred ministers by the sacrament of holy orders. They are thus consecrated and deputed so that, each according to his own grade, they may serve the people of God by a new and specific title. . . .
>
> Those who are constituted in the order of the episcopate or the presbyterate receive the mission and capacity to act in the person of Christ the Head, whereas deacons are empowered to serve the people of God in the ministries of the liturgy, the word and charity.

In summary, it may be said that according to the Code, some among the Christian faithful, by divine institution, become deacons through sacramental ordination in which an indelible character is received.

Deacons, through this consecration, share in the governance of the church ("consecrated and deputed so that, . . . they may serve the people of God"), and act with a special strength (or, as LG 29 refers to it, the sacramental grace of the sacrament) to serve in the threefold ministry of teaching, sanctifying, and governing.

The comparable Eastern canons 323 and 324 provide an interesting contrast. Canon 323 §1 states, "Clerics, who are also called sacred ministers, are Christian faithful who, chosen by the competent ecclesiastical authority, are deputed through a gift of the Holy Spirit received in sacred ordination to be ministers of the Church participating in the mission and power of Christ, the Pastor." Again, clerics are identified as Christian faithful who assume additional responsibility through ordination, and they are described as "participating in the mission and power of Christ, the Pastor." In both codes, therefore, is the explicit reference that all clerics, regardless of order, have a role in governance, a fact made explicit in the 1983 code, cc. 129 and 274: "Those who have received sacred orders are qualified, according to the norm of the prescripts of the law, for the power of governance, which exists in the Church by divine institution and is also called the power of jurisdiction" (129 §1); "[o]nly clerics can obtain offices for whose exercise the power of orders or the power of ecclesiastical governance is required" (274 §1). Canon 743 of the Eastern Code describes this effect in this way: "Through sacramental ordination celebrated by a bishop in virtue of the working of the Holy Spirit, sacred ministers are constituted, who are endowed with the function and power the Lord granted to his apostles, and in varying degrees share in the proclamation of the gospel, shepherding and sanctifying the people of God."

Ordination is about relationships, and not simply about an individual's personal empowerment. There is the relationship of the ordinand to Christ, to the ordaining bishop, to the rest of the order into which the ordinand is being incorporated and to the entire people of God. Incardination, another canonical effect of ordination, establishes these relationships within a particular church. Canon 266 specifies, "Through the reception of the diaconate, a person becomes a cleric and is incardinated in the particular church or personal prelature for whose service he has been advanced" (§1). Properly understood, sacramental ordination is at least as much about what is happening in the local church as it is about what is happening with the ordinand.

When looking specifically into the canonical references to the deacon's role in the *munus regendi*, we have already examined the notion of "the care of souls" as mentioned in LG 29 and the Code. One area of governance that we have not yet examined, since it is an extraordinary situation not associated with every deacon, is the servant-leadership provided by some deacons in parishes without a resident pastor or parochial vicar. We shall examine it briefly, however, since increasing numbers of deacons are serving in what have become known informally as "Canon 517 §2 parishes." However, perhaps even more significant and pertinent to our aims here is the insight that is offered about the nature of the diaconate that emerged during the development of the canon itself.

## The Deacon and Canon 517 §2

This canon provides for the pastoral care of parishes when insufficient numbers of presbyters are available. For that reason, it is necessary to examine the development of this canon closely. The provisions of c. 517 §2 are new in the 1983 Code and it has no parallel in the Eastern Code:

> If, because of a lack of priests, the diocesan bishop has decided that participation in the exercise of the pastoral care of a parish is to be entrusted to a deacon, to another person who is not a priest, or to a community of persons, he is to appoint some priest who, provided with the powers and faculties of a pastor, is to direct the pastoral care.

On the one hand, examining the role of the deacon under this canon may seem to place undue emphasis on an extraordinary circumstance, rather than an ordinary diaconal function. However, as discussed below, deacons are given a definite precedence under the law and in recent Vatican documents for this ministry, and our purpose is to investigate why this is the case.

The goal of the canon is to ensure that full pastoral care is provided through the assignment of pastors to every parish, even when those parishes may not have the presence of a resident pastor. The history of the development of this canon is illustrative.[11] The context of the canon is the need for some person to provide for the *cura animarum* in each parish. Since only a priest can supply *full* care of souls, provisions must be made to provide some priest with that responsibility, even if that priest is not resident in the parish. Furthermore, if the priest is not resident, someone else must coordinate day-to-day pastoral life. Consequently, the canon is found in the chapter dealing with pastors, parishes, and parochial vicars. From the beginning of the Code revision process the possibility was considered that there might be insufficient numbers of presbyters to pastor every parish. The initial drafts of the canon focused less on who would actually provide daily pastoral leadership to such a parish, but on the priest who would be appointed to oversee (but not pastor) the parish. In some dioceses, for example, a priest (sometimes the vicar general) oversees all parishes under the care of a person other than a presbyter. The purpose of the canon is to provide the parish with a priest to oversee the pastoral care of a parish. It is only in the subordinate clause of the canon that is found the provision of on-scene pastoral leadership by someone other than a priest. While the language of the canon continued to evolve throughout the years of the drafting process, this has remained the principal concern of the canon.

Deacons were first mentioned in connection with the canon in May 1980. "If, because of a lack of priests, the diocesan bishop has determined that participation in the exercise of the pastoral care of a parish is to be entrusted to some deacon or even (*etiam*) to a lay member of the Christian faithful or to a group of them, he is to appoint. . . ."[12] John McCarthy captures the significance: "This revised text is significant because it not only mentions explicitly the possibility of a deacon functioning as the on-site assistant but, by inclusion of the word 'even' (*etiam*), seems to suggest that a deacon would be preferable in that role to a lay person or group of persons."[13] Later discussions confirmed that the exercise of such a ministry by laypersons is always an *extraordinary and temporary* situation, inferring that a cleric (namely, the deacon) would do so in an *ordinary and permanent* manner. In some drafts, the reference to the deacon was removed as unnecessary for the same reason: "Deacons always have, in a certain ordinary and permanent way, 'participation in the exercise of the pastoral care of a parish.'"[14] Eventually, however, and with no explanation, the reference to deacons was included in the final redaction of the canon, and the original distinction between clergy and laity was removed. McCarthy concludes reasonably that "deacons have priority as a consequence of ordination,"[15] an ordination that gives deacons a certain ordinary and permanent responsibility for pastoral care.

Recent Vatican documents reach the same conclusion. The 1997 interdicasterial instruction, *Ecclesiae de Mysterio*,[16] addresses the provisions of c. 517 §2 in part as follows:

> The right understanding and application of this canon . . . requires that this exceptional provision be used only with strict adherence to conditions contained in it. These are:
>
> a) *a shortage of priests* [emphasis in text] and not for reasons of convenience or ambiguous "advancement of the laity," etc.;
>
> b) this is *a share in the exercise of the pastoral care* [emphasis in text] and not de facto directing, coordinating, moderating or governing the parish; these competencies, according to the canon, are the competencies of a presbyter alone.
>
> Because these are exceptional cases, before employing them, other possibilities should be considered, e.g., using the services of retired presbyters still capable of such service, or entrusting several parishes to one priest or to "several priests jointly." *In any event, the preference which this canon gives to deacons cannot be overlooked* [emphasis added].[17]

In 1998, the Congregation for the Clergy was even more emphatic. In dealing with this canon, the Congregation asserted:

> Where permanent deacons participate in the pastoral care of parishes which do not, because of a shortage, have the immediate benefit of a parish priest, they always have precedence over the nonordained faithful. . . . When deacons are available, participation in the pastoral care of the faithful may not be entrusted to a lay person or to a community of lay persons. (DMLPD 41)

Throughout this Code revision process, then, there is an underlying presupposition that deacons exercise some *ordinary* responsibility for the care of souls that goes beyond the responsibility of the baptized faithful. The deacon's exercise of governance is limited to offices and functions not requiring "the priestly character" such as pastor or parochial vicar. And yet, the deacon is given a certain canonical precedence over the laity when pastoral leadership is required in the absence of a presbyter. The nature of this preference demands attention and further research that goes far beyond the scope of the current project.

This chapter has sought to demonstrate one major point: that deacons, by virtue of their ordination, exercise a particular public leadership role in the church, a role that is well documented in the church's magisterial documents and in canon law. In the remaining chapters we will explore the many ways in which this governance might be exercised.

# PART II

# The Mission of Mercy

## The Mission, the Deacon, and "Concrete Consequences"

The drama of the account speaks for itself. In Luke's account, Jesus began his public ministry by proclaiming his mission. His mission becomes ours. Deacons, as participants in the apostolic ministry, take on a particular obligation through ordination for seeing that this mission is carried out.

> When he came to Nazareth, where he had been brought up, he went to the synagogue on the sabbath day, as was his custom. He stood up to read, and the scroll of the prophet Isaiah was given to him. He unrolled the scroll and found the place where it was written:
>
> "The Spirit of the Lord is upon me,
>   because he has anointed me
>     to bring good news to the poor.
> He has sent me to proclaim release to the captives
>   and recovery of sight to the blind,
>     to let the oppressed go free,
>   to proclaim the year of the Lord's favor."
>
> And he rolled up the scroll, gave it back to the attendant, and sat down. The eyes of all in the synagogue were fixed on him. Then he began to say to them, "Today this scripture has been fulfilled in your hearing." (Luke 4:16-21)

Anointed by the Spirit, to bring good news to the poor, release for those bound, sight to the sightless, and freedom for all who are oppressed, and over all of that, a proclamation of God's love and mercy. Everything proclaimed by Christ bespeaks the mercy of God.

Pope Francis began the Bull of Indiction for the holy year of mercy by proclaiming, "Jesus Christ is the face of God's Mercy,"[1] and this is readily apparent in Jesus' words in that synagogue in Nazareth. Francis further cites St. John Paul II: "The Church lives an authentic life when she professes and proclaims mercy—the most stupendous attribute of the Creator and of the Redeemer—and when she brings people close to the sources of the Savior's mercy, of which she is the trustee and dispenser."[2] In part 2, all that is presented is through the lens of God's mercy, since that mercy is the foundation for all of our efforts at charity and justice.

What Jesus proclaims in the synagogue is simple: God's mercy is not a theoretical notion. It is practical, hands-on, and specific. It is where "rubber meets road." It is precisely in this dimension that the Order of Deacons finds its true focus and its fullest expression. The deacon is called, ordained, and sent to proclaim the Good News to those he knows are suffering because he has been with them in the streets, to place the water of that struggling humanity into the wine that becomes Christ during Eucharist, and then return to the streets to lead efforts to channel God's mercy to those still suffering. German theologian Herbert Vorgrimler observed, "In his person, the deacon makes it clear that the liturgy must have concrete consequences in the world with all its needs, and that work in the world that is done in the spirit of charity has a spiritual dimension."[3] When all is said and done, that's what this whole book is about. Pope Francis refers to mercy as the "beating heart" of the Gospel, and deacons are part of the apostolic ministry devoted to serving that ministry in real, particular, and practical terms. In doing this, the deacon is not simply a well-intentioned disciple, but an apostle of mercy. "All that the deacon does is done *as* a member of the hierarchy, of the *clerus*; . . . the deacon is one of the sacramentally ordained. . . . Sacramental ordination asks for and effects in deacons the grace to perform this service."[4]

Each of the succeeding chapters offers suggestions for the deacon's exercise of a ministry of mercy, charity, and justice. They are not intended to be exhaustive but suggestive. It remains for each deacon everywhere, and all deacons collectively, to chart his own course. We must do this, however, not based on our own plan, skills, or needs, but on the needs of others. The question is not, "What will I do?" The question must be, "What does this person need right here, right now, and what will I do—concretely—to help meet that need?"

# CHAPTER 5

## Pope Francis, Deacons, and the Gospel of Mercy

On Wednesday, March 13, 2013, I was at my desk in the diocesan offices. As a student of the church as well as a deacon, I had been asked many times over the preceding weeks—as most of us were asked, I'm sure—who I thought would be the next pope. I usually tried some clever response, such as the old Italian adage, "He who enters the conclave as pope, leaves it a cardinal," because it is foolish to try to predict the outcome of a conclave.

And yet, there was a particular excitement in the air. Following Pope Benedict's stunning announcement of his retirement from the papal office—an act of profound humility and courage as well as one of stupendous historical significance that will be perhaps his most profound legacy—everyone could feel that just about anything could happen now. After all, if the pope could resign, how would that change the map of the papacy? If the pope could resign, how might that change the calculus of the conclave? Consider just one example: the age of candidates. Pope St. John XXIII was seventy-six when he was elected in October 1958; he turned seventy-seven the following month. At the time, he was believed to be the oldest pope ever elected. From the moment of his election, it was a given that he was not going to be around long, and that he had been elected, at least partially, to serve as an "interim" pope following the lengthy papacy of his predecessor Pope Pius XII. He used to quip that people often made the mistake of thinking that since he wouldn't be around long, that he wouldn't do anything while he was there! He, of course, proved those people wrong. But in most conclaves, certain candidates are ruled out because they are considered too old for the job: they might be too frail or in ill health for the burdens of the office, or they might simply succumb to old age before being able to accomplish anything.

Such was the case in 2013. There was considerable speculation in the press about various candidates, and some were considered unlikely due to their age. But Pope Benedict's decision changed that picture stunningly. Now an older man might be elected and then have the option, like Benedict, to retire in order to permit another to step into the shoes of the fisherman. Papal transitions no longer had to follow the precedent of centuries but could actually be done in a more orderly manner. So, as the cardinals processed into the Sistine Chapel that March, it seemed like just about anything could happen. And it did.

While sitting at my desk, watching the coverage from Rome, the announcement was made by the cardinal deacon: "Habemus Papam!" Who was it going to be? And out walked Jorge Mario Bergoglio, the retired archbishop of Buenos Aires, as the new Bishop of Rome (the term he has consistently preferred), and most of us went scrambling to find out more about him. What a wonderful and exciting time it has been since that night, finding out more about him!

I did what many of us do these days when we want to find out something quickly: I googled him. The very first image that popped up on the screen was the now-famous image of then-Archbishop Bergoglio washing the feet of AIDS patients (men, women, and children). What a wonderful image, I thought, and then leaned forward to study the picture more closely. I even zoomed in to make sure: the archbishop was indeed wearing his stole in the fashion of a Latin-rite deacon! In fact, it was quite clear that this had been a deliberate act. It was clearly a priest's stole that had been consciously rearranged after he had removed his chasuble in order to wash the patients' feet. Think of that: the new pope saw this ministry as properly diaconal, so much so that he intentionally, carefully, and deliberatively rearranged his stole to communicate that fact. I could not remember ever seeing any priest or bishop do such a thing before, and it left me stunned. Truly this new pope "valued" the diaconate, and saw the washing of the feet of the poor and the outcast as a principal expression of mercy and the diaconal ministry. So, my first impression of the pope was that he was truly a deacon-pope. Meanwhile, on the screen, this shy, humble man simply greeted the Roman crowd with a "Buona sera" and, in yet another remarkable moment, asked the people to pray for him and bowed deeply for a time as they did so. Only then did he put on his stole and give his first blessing to the people as pope.

Every so often, some deacons will express a wish that Pope Francis would address deacons directly, or that he would speak about our ministry. While that would certainly be affirming and welcomed, it seems that we have in Francis a pope who prefers actions to words. This is by no means a criticism of any of his predecessors, not in the least! Every pope brings a particular frame of reference to the ministry of Peter, their own strengths and talents. Pope St. John XXIII was a deeply spiritual, joy-filled, and inspirational person, but he was not particularly strong at administration; by contrast, Pope Paul VI was a gifted administrator but sometimes struggled in other areas. Pope St. John Paul II was a gifted and energetic orator and pastor when he was elected, a brilliant philosopher; Pope Benedict was a gifted professor of theology who was often uncomfortable in large crowds. In the case of Pope Francis, he too is a learned man, but for him, the emphasis is on concrete action. In this dimension as well, then, we find a model for our own diaconal ministry. There are indeed many ways to serve: in the pulpit and classroom, through the liturgy and sacraments, and in charity and justice. But the test of such service, the pope is consistently reminding us, is this: how is what I am doing helping someone else in concrete and specific ways?

In addition to his daily homilies and his catecheses at the Wednesday public audiences, we have two principal documents from Pope Francis that give us insight into our role as deacons, serving charity and justice. First, there is the first major document of Francis's papacy, *Evangelii Gaudium* (The Joy of the Gospel). I agree with other commentators that this document is a road map to his papacy. The second document is the Bull of Indiction for the holy year on mercy, *Misericordiae Vultus* (The Face of Mercy). This document provides even more specific and practical applications of themes raised by *Evangelii Gaudium* (EG). Let us consider each briefly through the lens of *diakonia* and, in particular, the ministry of charity and justice.

### *Evangelii Gaudium*: Lessons for Deacons, Part 1

This is not the place for an in-depth analysis of the entire exhortation. The entire document is a stunningly "diaconal" text, and the comprehensive section on the homily alone is a wonderful resource. However, I want to focus on two particular sections of the document of particular interest for deacons in their exercise of a ministry of charity and justice. In this section we will review what the pope refers to as the "temptations faced by pastoral workers" (sections 76–109). Here, we look at the person of the deacon-as-pastoral-worker, not at the work itself. We will look at the ministry itself in the following section, drawn from chapter 4 of the exhortation, "The Social Dimension of Evangelization" (sections 176–258). Following each "temptation" there are some "questions for reflection" to aid in our own ongoing discernment. It is frequently observed that we do not assess a deacon's ministry solely on what he does but on who he is. I believe that by focusing first on these "temptations and challenges" we place our first emphasis on the identity of the deacon before then turning to the ministry of the deacon in charity and justice.

## "Temptations Faced by Pastoral Workers"

By pastoral workers the pope means just that: *anyone* who is serving others in the name of the church "from bishops down to those who provide the most humble and hidden services" (EG 76). His concern is for the challenges all of us face, regardless of our particular ministries. Let's examine the pope's comments as they might apply especially to deacons.

The first concern addressed by the pope is with pressures that can "limit, condition and ultimately harm us." He continues, "We need to create spaces where pastoral workers can be helped and healed, 'places where faith itself in the crucified and risen Jesus is renewed, where the most profound questions and daily concerns are shared, where deeper discernment about our experiences and life itself is undertaken in the light of the Gospel" (EG 77). Even before he gets to the actual "temptations," he raises the fundamental concern that those who serve need to be cared for as well, particularly our spiritual and emotional health.

*Reflection*
1. Are we in regular spiritual direction?
2. How often do we take time for personal prayer and reflection?
3. Do we regularly (at least annually) participate in a retreat?

4. For married deacons: Have the stresses of ministry begun to affect your family life adversely? Are you able to take time to focus on family relationships?

We can perhaps take a lesson from the safety briefing we hear before a flight. If the oxygen masks fall, we are to get a mask on ourselves first before we help others around us. A more traditional way to express this same idea is in the axiom, *Nemo dat quod non habet*: No one gives what one does not have. If our mission is to introduce others to Christ, we must take care that our own relationship with Christ exists and is strong. Whether it is termed clergy burnout or simple fatigue, it can be one of the easiest traps to fall into. If "charity begins at home," perhaps it can be said that the deacon's ministry of charity and justice needs to be well grounded on the deacon's own physical, emotional, and spiritual health.

### Temptation #1: Challenge of a Missionary Spirituality

The pope highlights a temptation among many pastoral workers, "including consecrated men and women," to have an "inordinate concern for their personal freedom" and individualism, resulting in an approach to ministry that sees ministry as "a mere appendage to their life, as if it were not part of their very identity." He criticizes this approach to spirituality that consists of certain "religious exercises" but still does not engage others in any meaningful way. He warns against "a heightened individualism, a crisis of identity and a cooling of fervor. These are three evils which fuel one another" (EG 78).

As another challenge within this temptation, the pope refers to a "marked skepticism . . . and a certain cynicism" about the church and her teachings. This results in an "inferiority complex" that relativizes their very Christian identity. In a desire to be like everyone else, the pastoral worker winds up unhappy and unable to be a missionary evangelist. Finally, the pope develops the theme of relativism even further. He refers to it as a "practical relativism," which is even more dangerous than "doctrinal relativism." Practical relativism "consists in acting as if God did not exist, making decisions as if the poor did not exist, setting goals as if others did not exist, working as if people who have not received the Gospel did not exist."

It is striking that even some who clearly have solid doctrinal and spiritual convictions frequently fall into a lifestyle which leads to an attachment to financial security, or to a desire for power or human glory at all cost, rather than giving their lives to others in mission. Let us not allow ourselves to be robbed of missionary enthusiasm! (EG 79–80)

### Reflection

1. Deacons are charged at ordination: "Believe what you read, teach what you believe, and practice what you teach." Do we still believe what we read or, as the pope cautions, have we become skeptical or even cynical about the message?
2. Do we truly teach what we believe, or do we water down the message in order to be popular or to please others?
3. Do we indeed put into practice what we believe and what we teach? Even Shakespeare understood the integrity involved here: "Suit the action to the word, the word to the action." Perhaps over time, the temptation to "practical relativism" has affected us and we have lost the missionary enthusiasm the pope mentions.

### Temptation #2: Selfishness and Spiritual Sloth

The next temptation cited by Pope Francis is for pastoral workers to see their ministry as one activity in their lives among many, a temptation to guard themselves and wind up "in a state of paralysis." He cautions against undertaking activity "without a spirituality which would permeate it and make it pleasurable. As a result, work becomes more tiring than necessary." He suggests many reasons for this, but it can lead to a "tomb psychology" that "slowly transforms Christians into mummies in a museum" (EG 81–83). Pastoral workers then lose heart and stop altogether.

It is still common to hear the ministry of deacons referred to as a "part-time" commitment. Very often pastors will fall into this error, and certainly a number of parishioners perceive the diaconate in this way. After all, they say, the deacon has family and work responsibilities that keep him from "full-time ministry." John Paul II preached powerfully against such a misconception. Here is one example. In 1995 he addressed a joint plenarium of the cardinal-members of the Congregations for Clergy and for Catholic Education as they were beginning their work on the two documents that would be known as the Directory for the Ministry and Life of Permanent Deacons and the Basic Norms for the Formation of Permanent Deacons:

> [The] essential characteristics of his ecclesial vocation must pervade his readiness to give himself to the Church and must be reflected in his outward behavior. The Church expects of the permanent deacon a faithful witness to his ministerial state. The exercise of the diaconal ministry—like that of other ministries in the Church—requires of all deacons, celibate or married, a spiritual attitude of total dedication. Although in certain cases it is necessary to make the ministry of the diaconate compatible with other obligations, to think of oneself and to act in practice as a "part-time deacon" would make no sense. The deacon is not a part-time employee or ecclesiastical official, but a minister of the Church. His is not a profession, but a mission! It is the circumstances of his life—prudently evaluated by the candidate himself and by the bishop, before ordination—which should, if necessary, be adapted to the exercise of his ministry by facilitating it in every way.[1]

### Reflection

1. As deacons, do we sometimes fall into the trap of thinking of ourselves as part-time ministers? Is diaconate simply one activity among many in our lives?
2. Is our spirituality one "which permeates [ministry] and makes it pleasurable"?
3. Pope Francis often contrasts "the joy of the Gospel" with the loss of that joy due to an inner weariness, depression, and melancholy. In our own ministries, are we still full of joy and enthusiasm?
4. Pope John Paul II, in the quote above, states that the diaconal ministry is a mission, not a profession, and that it is everything else ("the circumstances of his life") that is to be adapted to the exercise of ministry, not the other way around. In our own experience, do we adapt our lives to ministry, or adapt our ministry to fit our lives?

### Temptation #3: A Sterile Pessimism

Pope Francis consistently turns to Pope John XXIII, and he does so again here as he warns against losing the joy of the Gospel because of "the evils of our world—and those of the Church" (EG 84). He reminds us that the light of the Spirit will always radiate within the darkness.

It is here that the pope cites Pope John's opening address to the Second Vatican Council. Pope John refers to those with whom he was serving who could see "nothing but prevarication and ruin" and how he disagreed with "those prophets of doom who are always forecasting disaster as though the end of the world were at hand." However, Pope John speaks of Divine Providence leading us to a "new order of human relations" and that "everything, even human setbacks, leads to the greater good of the Church." Pope Francis picks up on this theme, referring to a temptation to "a defeatism which turns us into querulous and disillusioned pessimists, 'sourpusses'" (EG 85).

### Reflection
1. Do we suffer from this kind of pessimism and defeatism? Would our parishioners and others perhaps see us as "sourpusses" when it comes to ministry?
2. The challenges of today's world can seem overwhelming, but do we agree with St. John XXIII's observation that "everything, even human setbacks, leads to the greater good of the Church"? How does that find expression in our own ministries?

### Temptation #4: Isolation vs. New Relationships in Christ
The pope returns to his concerns over a temptation to isolationism. He alludes to modern technology in which people have a greater ability to connect with so many others, but also the impression that we can turn off and shut down from relationships with the flip of a switch. Instead of achieving greater possibilities for encounter and communication, we can find ourselves turning inward and "self-enclosed" and selfish. The pope speaks of a temptation to isolate ourselves with perhaps a small circle of friends, thereby "renouncing the realism of the social aspect of the Gospel."

> For just as some people want a purely spiritual Christ, without flesh and without the cross, they also want their interpersonal relationships provided by sophisticated equipment, by screens and systems which can be turned on and off on command. . . . True faith in the incarnate Son of God is inseparable from self-giving, from membership in the community, from service, from reconciliation with others. The Son of God, by becoming flesh, summoned us to the revolution of tenderness. (EG 88)

## Reflection

1. What can we do, in concrete terms, to overcome contemporary isolationism?
2. In our own lives, do we fall victim to this temptation? Being engaged in public ministry might lead to a desire to "disconnect" at times. Has this led to a gradual disengagement from others?
3. How might deacons participate in Christ's "revolution of tenderness"?

### Temptation #5: Spiritual Worldliness

At first, the title the pope gives to this temptation can seem a bit hard to define, but the description he gives clears things up nicely. The pope is clearly passionate about the dangers of this temptation, and he minces no words in his criticism of it; for this reason, I offer a lengthy quotation from this section. He speaks of a contemporary form of Gnosticism, "a purely subjective faith whose only interest is a certain experience or set of ideas and bits of information which are meant to console and enlighten, but which ultimately keep one imprisoned in his or her own thoughts and feelings" (EG 93). It is also found in

> the self-absorbed promethean neopelagianism of those who ultimately trust only in their own powers and feel superior to others because they observe certain rules or remain intransigently faithful to a particular Catholic style from the past. A supposed soundness of doctrine or discipline leads instead to a narcissistic and authoritarian elitism, whereby instead of evangelizing, one analyzes and classifies others, and instead of opening the door to grace, one exhausts his or her energies in inspecting and verifying. . . .
>
> This insidious worldliness is evident in a number of attitudes which appear opposed, yet all have the same pretense of "taking over the space of the Church." In some people we see an ostentatious preoccupation for the liturgy, for doctrine and for the Church's prestige, but without any concern that the Gospel has a real impact on God's faithful people and the concrete needs of the present time. In this way, the life of the Church turns into a museum piece of something which is the property of a select few. . . . It can also lead to a business mentality, caught up with management, statistics, plans and evaluations whose principal beneficiary is not God's people but the Church as an institution. The mark of Christ, incarnate, crucified and risen, is not present; closed and elite groups are formed, and no

effort is made to go forth and seek out those who are distant or the immense multitudes who thirst for Christ. (EG 94–95)

Calling all of this a "tremendous corruption disguised as a good," the way to avoid this temptation is by "making the Church constantly go out from herself, keeping her mission focused on Jesus Christ, and her commitment to the poor" (EG 97).

### Reflection
1. How often might we succumb to the temptation to focus more on certain public expressions of the church but without a concrete appreciation for the real lives of the people we serve?
2. Do we sometimes focus on "preserving" the church at the expense of "putting out into the deep" to seek those who are searching desperately for meaning in their lives? As St. Paul reminded the Philippians, Christ himself did not grasp his divinity but let it go, emptying himself. Can we say the same?

### Temptation #6: Warring among Ourselves
The temptation to spiritual worldliness leads to the next temptation, that of warring among ourselves. It "leads some Christians to war with other Christians. . . . Some are even no longer content to live as part of the greater Church community but stoke a spirit of exclusivity, creating an 'inner circle.' Instead of belonging to the whole Church in all its rich variety, they belong to this or that group which thinks itself different or special" (EG 98). The pope asks us all to be an "attractive witness of fraternal communion" (EG 99).

Anyone who has journeyed into various media outlets or online has experienced the type of polarizing warfare of words going on between various factions within the church. Not merely content with disagreement over ideas, principles, and practices, one frequently reads blistering attributions of motives or sinfulness in those of opposing "camps." And then, of course, there is the very literal, longstanding, and horrific warfare that goes on between regional groups of Christians against each other. The challenge is to respond to Jesus' prayer that what should be our most defining public characteristic is our love for one another.

### Reflection

1. How are disagreements handled within our community, including our parish community?
2. As deacons, what are we doing to overcome polarization within the community, or do we find ourselves at times favoring one group over against another?
3. The Second Vatican Council (*Lumen Gentium* 18) teaches that all the ordained exist for one reason: to build up the Body of Christ. When considering our own efforts in ministry, are we serving to build up or to tear down? How do we reach out to those with whom we might disagree or who disagree with us?

### Other Pastoral Challenges

Although he does not list these challenges as temptations, Pope Francis nonetheless presents four additional concerns: the role of the laity in general, the role of women in particular, youth, and vocations to the priesthood and consecrated life.

The pope acknowledges the great presence of the laity in service within the structures of the church; he decries the fact that many laypeople do not exercise a transformative influence in the social, political, and economic spheres. "The formation of the laity and the evangelization of professional and intellectual life represent a significant challenge" (EG 102).

Again acknowledging the existing and extensive presence and ministry of women in the church, Pope Francis writes, "We need to create still broader opportunities for a more incisive female presence in the Church. . . . This presents a great challenge to pastors and theologians, who are in a position to recognize more fully what this entails with regard to the possible role of women in decision making in different areas of the Church's life" (EG 103–4).

In the area of outreach to youth, the pope applauds the many associations and youth movements but cautions that these efforts must be better incorporated into the overall pastoral life of the entire church. And in the area of vocations to the priesthood and consecrated life, while acknowledging the positive efforts of many communities to foster vocations, he also warns that a shortage of priests does not justify a lessening of standards. "Seminaries cannot accept candidates on the basis of any motivation whatsoever, especially if those motivations have to do with affective insecurity or the pursuit of power, human glory or economic well-being" (EG 107).

He ends, as always, striking a positive note: "Challenges exist to be overcome! Let us be realists, but without losing our joy, our boldness and our hope-filled commitment. Let us not allow ourselves to be robbed of missionary vigor!" (EG 109).

### *Reflection*
1. As deacons, are we involved in addressing any of these four challenges in specific, concrete ways? What are they?
2. How do we, as deacons, approach challenges? Do we share in the pope's bold optimism and vigor? Do we still exhibit our own joy over the Gospel, despite the temptations and challenges we face?

## *Evangelii Gaudium*: **Lessons for Deacons, Part 2**

Because subsequent chapters will develop the deacon's role in charity and justice in more detail, this section can be somewhat brief. I include it because it forms the climax of *Evangelii Gaudium*, and we must see it as the foundational vision for what will come in *Misericordiae Vultus*. Chapter 4 of *Evangelii Gaudium* consists of four sections: (1) the communal and societal repercussions of the kerygma, (2) the inclusion of the poor in society, (3) the common good and peace in society, and (4) social dialogue as a contribution to peace.

"Christ has died; Christ is risen; Christ will come again!" The ancient, fundamental proclamation (*kerygma*) of Christian faith is simple and direct, but the import of that proclamation is profound. Pope Francis likewise begins this section with a simple statement: "To evangelize is to make the kingdom of God present in our world." He continues, "at the very heart of the Gospel is life in community and engagement with others. . . . To believe that the Son of God assumed our human flesh means that each human person has been taken up into the very heart of God" (EG 176–78). What I find illustrative here is the reference to "the heart of the Gospel." In *Misericordiae Vultus*, the pope extends his theme: "The Church is commissioned to announce the mercy of God, the beating heart of the Gospel, which in its own way must penetrate the heart and mind of every person. The Spouse of Christ must pattern her behavior after the Son of God who went out to everyone without exception" (12). Every person has been drawn into the heart of God where mercy awaits.

Pope Francis devotes the rest of this section stressing the communal dimensions of this message. In a particularly strong passage, he points out that "the Gospel is not merely about our personal relationship with God. Nor should our loving response to God be seen simply as an accumulation of small personal gestures to individuals in need, a kind of 'charity à la carte,' or a series of acts aimed solely at easing our conscience. . . . Both Christian preaching and life, then, are meant to have an impact on society" (EG 180).

Deacons, therefore, as apostolic leaders in *diakonia*, have a special responsibility for the very implementation of these relationships. Mercy, charity, and justice are not optional additions to Christianity; they are at the very heart of who we are as Christians and as deacons. Most deacons have heard the expression, sometimes said by another deacon, but sometimes spoken about deacons, "Oh, he's just a deacon." Indeed, being "just a deacon" means everything in light of the *kerygma* of Christianity. Those "concrete consequences" spoken of by Vorgrimler find an echo in Pope Francis: "The Church's teachings concerning contingent situations are subject to new and further developments and can be open to discussion, yet we cannot help but be concrete— without presuming to enter into details—lest the great social principles remain mere generalities which challenge no one" (EG 182). The deacons of the church, however, along with our lay sisters and brothers, *may* enter into the details, which transforms principles to action, generalities into specifics.

Pope Francis highlights the fact that Christ himself was poor, and that he "was always close to the poor and the outcast." Once again he repeats his theme that our relationship with the poor is not some optional aspect of Christianity. "We incarnate the duty of hearing the cry of the poor when we are deeply moved by the suffering of others. Let us listen to what God's word teaches us about mercy, and allow that word to resound in the life of the Church. The Gospel tells us: 'Blessed are the merciful, because they shall obtain mercy' (Mt 5:7)" (EG 193). Here we find again Pope Francis's theme of mercy, which he will develop further in *Misericordiae Vultus*. He observes that the preferential option for the poor to the charity of the church "is why I want a Church which is poor and for the poor." This is not simply a charitable impulse, but because the poor—in their poverty—can teach us about the suffering Christ, therefore, "we need to let ourselves be evangelized by them" (EG 198).

The final two sections of the chapter further explicate the implications of the first two. In the pope's language about the common good, the nature of peace, and social dialogue we find a wonderful explication of traditional church teaching, especially the teaching contained in the documents of the Second Vatican Council and, in particular, in part 2 of the Pastoral Constitution on the Church in the Modern World (*Gaudium et Spes*). We shall return to these themes in subsequent chapters.

## Conclusion: Deacons in Action

Deacons are the guardians and the heralds of the good news of Jesus Christ, charged as such at ordination. Deacons proclaim the Gospel, deacons hold the Gospel book open tentlike over a newly ordained bishop, and deacons preach the Gospel in word and in action. The deacon is charged with this responsibility to symbolize the connection between Christ the Word of God and the "concrete consequences" of that Gospel. Therefore, deacons and the ministry of charity and justice are at the heart of the joy of the Gospel and in the sharing of God's mercy. Both of the pope's documents, when read through the lens of *diakonia*, are indeed charters for the deacon's ministry.

# CHAPTER 6

# The Deacon and the Rights of All

## Guidelines for Diaconal Leadership

In seeking the concrete applications of all that has been said about deacons, mercy, charity, and justice, we return to the question of leadership and governance by deacons. We have discussed the general principles of such leadership; now we turn our attention to an aspect of that leadership: the rights of all persons. In carrying out his ministries, the deacon must keep the rights of all in mind. The late canonist Fr. James Provost wrote,

> Concern for rights is traditionally a central concern of governance. . . . The Catholic Church today has come to a renewed understanding of the rights of people within its communion. The social teaching of the Church has emphasized the importance of human rights. The synods of bishops in 1971 and 1974 recognized that this teaching applies also within the Church and not just in a secular context. The new code specifically addresses the rights and obligations common to all the Christian faithful (cc. 208-223).[1]

Provost developed twelve rules for diocesan governance,[2] which I have adapted slightly to apply to deacons, and the notion of human rights is the cornerstone of his rules. After reviewing them briefly, we will turn to a review of one of the most significant papal encyclicals ever written, especially in terms of human rights, St. John XXIII's landmark *Pacem in Terris*. To reiterate: my purpose with this focus on canon law and rights is to ground the deacon's ministry within the framework of the instruments available to support that ministry.

Here are Provost's twelve guidelines, adapted slightly for diaconal leadership.

### 1. Be Always Vigilant for the Spiritual Purpose

Canon 1752, the last canon in the Code of Canon Law, says it well: "*Salus animarum suprema lex*": the salvation of souls is the highest law. As Provost points out, "it is not only a literary device with which the legislator concluded the new code . . . ; it reflects the very purpose of diocesan governance, which is ultimately spiritual" (ibid., 249). For deacons this is particularly good counsel. According to Cardinal Walter Kasper,

> The basic spiritual attitude of the deacon must make it clear that the Christian path is not an ascent or a triumphal march in glory, but a path that looks downward, following Jesus Christ, who descended from heaven. This "downwardly mobile career" is described in the Christological hymn in the Letter to the Philippians (2:6-11), which prescribes the basic Christian virtue, as the spiritual tradition teaches, namely, the attitude of humility, which is a willingness to serve. This must *a fortiori* be the basic attitude of the deacon.[3]

As we serve in any ministry, but perhaps most especially in ministries of mercy, charity, and justice, it can be easy to get so engrossed in the details of the service that we might lose sight of the ultimate purpose. While our functions in ministries of charity might seem identical to that of a social worker or a volunteer, there is a difference. What we do, we do as members of the clergy, representing the entire church. Deacons, as sharers in the apostolic ministry of the church, extend the reach and presence of the bishop. We act in the person of Christ and in the name of the church to free others for an even greater purpose. "The task [for the deacon] is to bring a healing that sets people free and empowers them to trust and so to serve and love others in their turn."[4]

### 2. Think with the Church

The well-known phrase from St. Ignatius of Loyola, *sentire cum Ecclesia*, applies to canon law as well. Provost writes, "Church law is to be interpreted in light of the teaching and new way of thinking characteristic of the Second Vatican Council."[5] We have already seen the importance of this new way of thinking (*novus habitus mentis*) and its impact on diaconal ministry. In all that deacons do, they must constantly keep in mind the full riches of the church's tradition, which can be a considerable challenge since many of the activities involving social concerns quickly involve the public and political sphere. Once that happens, the temptation to associate particular forms of ministry with secular political ideals can be great, with a temptation to side with one side or another. Our frame of reference, however, must always be "the teaching, witness and tradition of the Church" (ibid.).

### 3. Serve if You Would Lead

"Hierarchical authority is a service, directed toward the spiritual welfare of God's people. This service of leadership implies the development of the personality of the leader, attention to the common good, and commitment to the spiritual goal for which the Church exists" (ibid.). Provost here offers deacons a good summary of servant-leadership.

First is the fact that leaders are made, not born. Leadership skills can be learned; what's more, those skills can be adapted to varying pastoral circumstances. I have written elsewhere in greater detail than is possible here about the nature of diaconal leadership. As ordained ministers, deacons are to be leaders, which means formation (post pre- and post-ordination) must assist deacons in the development of their abilities and opportunities for leadership.

Second, Provost lists attention to the common good. What better priority to keep in mind for the deacon than that. As referenced before, Vatican II teaches that the whole point of our ordered ministries is to build up the Body of Christ: the common good of all. All of our judgments, then, can use that as a benchmark: Will an action or ministry proposed by a deacon serve to build up the Body, or not?

Third, Provost lists commitment to the spiritual goal for which the church exists. The salvation of souls should be at the heart of every minister.

### 4. Use the Power You Have

This rule, as described by Provost, refers primarily to the bishop, but it surely applies to all members of the church to some degree, including deacons. This is why I have included so much concerning our canon law: it is crucial that deacons understand the extent and the limits of the law as it applies to them, and how the law is properly interpreted. We should be competent to use all of our tools in the service of others and for the common good. Deacons receive power through their sacramental initiation as well as through sacramental ordination. The law continues to speak of powers of order and jurisdiction, and although far beyond the scope of this work, a word about the notion of "power" is in order.

Many today are hesitant to speak of "power" in an ecclesial context, thinking that it implies coercion or even abuse. From the earliest days of Christianity, there has been certain ambivalence about power-related language. It is often regarded with suspicion and fear that such concepts may even be at odds with Christian life itself. This concern is addressed directly by Agnes Cunningham:

> Our understanding of power and authority is based, more often than not, on two presuppositions. In the first place, we confuse power with its use or abuse and authority with its exercise or manipulation. In the second place, we tend at times to resent persons whose authority legitimizes their power in our regard and to be, perhaps unreasonably, captivated by those to whom authority is ascribed because of their display of native power in art or science, sports or entertainment, scholarship or one of the professions, business or communications.[6]

These legitimate concerns notwithstanding, power and its associated language remain part of the terms of discourse related to ministry and, in particular, the exercise of governance. Karl Rahner once offered two theological reasons why power must be understood properly:

> a) Power is one of the primary religious ideas; mankind's awareness of God is an awareness of him as powerful. Power is one of the first of God's attributes. That is also the case in OT and NT revelation. . . .
> b) A right attitude to power is fundamental in human social relations.[7]

God is the source of all power and in the Christian tradition "the sources of power derived from God are manifested historically through Jesus Christ and through the Holy Spirit."[8] This means that the church, in developing its own application and exercise of the ongoing presence and action of God's power, must do so in light of Christ's leadership and example. Canonist James Coriden puts it quite succinctly: "Power in the Church is power to serve."[9] Provost writes, "Failure to use power may not only be irresponsible, but damaging for the welfare of all the Church."

### 5. Empower the Church

Continuing this focus on sacramental empowerment, Provost writes, "All the Christian faithful, in virtue of Christ's action through the sacraments of initiation and charisms, participate in the mission which Christ gave the Church to accomplish in the world (c. 204, §I; AA, 3). To govern is to foster the common good; that is, to empower others to reach their potential, and thereby build up the Body of Christ."[10] Although when he wrote these words he was not referring specifically about deacons, certainly it applies totally and completely to the ministry of deacons vis-à-vis the ministry of charity and justice, as we have seen in detail in previous chapters.

### 6. Promote and Protect Rights

The notion of the rights of Christians has been imbedded in the Code of Canon Law itself, in addition to the documents that make up the rich magisterial tradition of the church's social teaching. "The obligations and rights of Christians are the context in which the hierarchical structure of the Church performs its Christ-given ministry of service" (ibid., 250). Because of this simple fact, in the next section of this chapter, we shall review some of the many rights found in our tradition; in particular, we will focus on the list of rights enumerated by Pope St. John XXIII in his encyclical *Pacem in Terris*. The deacon, especially in ministries of charity and justice, becomes an instrument of God's mercy and a guarantor of the rights of all they serve.

### 7. Consult When Making Decisions

In Provost's original listing, this rule focused on the technical requirements of the law for certain aspects of diocesan ministry that require consultation under the law. However, it applies equally well in the nontechnical sense. As the people of God, Mystical Body of Christ, and temple of the Holy Spirit, we believe that God's grace and wisdom come to all in some way. We are saved as members of the *qahal Yahweh*: the people called by God. So, "what touches all ought to be considered by all" (ibid.). Deacons should consider how best they too might consult in the course of their ministries. In addition, how might our ministries as deacons be exercised in community? No one serves in the church as a lone ranger. This can give us a sense of community and reassurance that we are not acting in isolation. We can benefit, grow, and be graced by the Spirit's working through each other.

### 8. Interpret the Law as It Is Meant to Be Interpreted

For some, laws seem beyond interpretation: they mean exactly and only what they say. However, every legal system needs interpretation; that's why every legal system has provisions for adjudication. In the case of canon law, Provost reminds us that "laws are made for God's people, not the people for laws. Indeed, no one is held to the impossible. The laws are therefore not meant to be interpreted in such a way as to make Christian living impossible, or to defeat the purpose of the salvation of souls. Anyone who administers the law interprets it" (ibid.).

Deacons administer the law in many ways: as they make decisions about aspects of sacramental life (qualifications of godparents at baptism, for example, or assisting parishioners seeking an annulment) and countless other ways in their various ministries in the streets, prisons, and other venues. Therefore, it is critically important that deacon candidates receive fundamental education in canon law, and that deacons continue to have opportunities to grow in their competence after ordination.

### 9. Be Generous

In this case, every word from Provost applies to the ministry of the deacon when dealing with the law:

> The law itself is generous, even to an accused person: when there has been a change in the law, the law which is more favorable to the accused is to be applied (c. 1313, §1). Traditionally, favors are to be expanded and burdensome matters restricted. Moreover, laws which establish a penalty, restrict the free exercise of rights, or which contain an exception to the law are to be interpreted strictly (c. 18). On the other hand, the law is generous in situations of doubt. (ibid.)

There can be a temptation in ministry to be rigorous in the application of the law when its proper interpretation tells us to be generous. This advice from Provost should be etched in the memory of every deacon: be generous in the application of the law.

### 10. Be Consistent

Once again, Provost could be speaking directly to deacons: "Effective governance is governance people can count on. What once seemed proper ought not suddenly to be presented as improper, nor should an opinion once adopted be changed to the detriment of another. Indeed, legal consistency is a characteristic of the Church's legislation, and should mark the service of those in diocesan governance" (ibid.).

### 11. Be Timely

"If justice delayed is justice denied, unnecessary delay in any aspect of governance can be harmful to people. The code sets various time limits to enforce timely governance; even where no limits are specified, sensitivity to the rights of persons calls for prudent timeliness" (ibid.).

### 12. Be Forthright

"The Church exists to bear witness to the gospel, to be a light to the nations. As with its teaching on social justice, so with forthrightness, the Church must practice what it preaches if it is to be a credible witness. Respecting proper confidentiality (c. 471) and preserving the privacy of others (c. 220) is important, but it cannot be an excuse for obscurantist practices or secretive governance. . . . The truth, after all, has nothing to fear from being proclaimed" (ibid.).

With these twelve rules or guidelines in mind, let us now turn to the rights of persons, the rights that deacons—and indeed all who serve—are ordained to assure. To do this, we turn to St. John XXIII and what has been called his "final will and testament," the encyclical *Pacem in Terris* (Peace on Earth).

## *Pacem in Terris*, **Deacons, and the Rights of Persons**

In reviewing these rights, we need to ask ourselves, *How will I, how will we as deacons* work to ensure, nurture, and promote these rights? As deacons serving in ministries focused on mercy, charity, justice, and peace, we must heed the caution of St. John Paul II that the *diakonia* of the church must be organized if it is to be effective. Part of understanding the ordering of *diakonia* will be to understand the rights and obligations of all persons.

### Background

Before turning to the encyclical itself, it is crucial to understand the context from which it emerged. In an earlier chapter, we examined the violent and deadly history of the first half of the twentieth century, and that must be recalled here. What St. John XXIII—and the majority of the bishops at the Second Vatican Council—was trying to do was nothing less than reforming and renewing the church to be a more effective witness of Christ in the contemporary world. This was seen as absolutely necessary if the world was to avoid continued violence in the future. The council was not merely a gathering to make modest changes to the liturgy and other aspects of church life; rather, its goal was far more extensive than that.

When the atomic bombs were dropped on Hiroshima and Nagasaki, the world became an even more dangerous place, as competition for that technology increased, especially between the two superpowers that had emerged following the war: the United States and the Soviet Union. Soon dubbed the Cold War (a terrible misnomer), conflicts continued around the world. As former empires continued to collapse following the war, colonial peoples claimed their independence, often after bitter fighting. Representatives from around the world gathered to form the United Nations. All of this continued throughout the 1950s, and when John XXIII was elected to the papacy in 1958. He himself had experienced World War I as a chaplain in the trenches, and World War II as the papal nuncio in Istanbul, from where he served both Turkey and Greece. He also worked with Jewish leaders throughout the war to save as many Jews as he could, with some estimates as high as 100,000 lives saved through his efforts. John was no stranger to the violent world of his time, and he realized that things were only going to get worse. What could the church do? In a phrase often associated with him, John observed that the role of any religion was "to make the human sojourn on earth less sad." To that end, he called the council.

By 1961, the Berlin Wall had been erected, becoming emblematic of the "Cold War" as the Eastern Bloc and the West, led by the United States, inched closer and closer to conflict. In October 1962, at exactly the same time the council was opening in Rome, both the Soviet Union and the United States conducted atmospheric nuclear tests. The week following, with the council barely getting started, the Cuban Missile Crisis took place. Because of prior dealings with both President Kennedy and Premier Khrushchev, Pope John was approached to work behind the scenes to mediate efforts at resolving the conflict before the world entered into a nuclear Third World War. Fortunately, largely through his efforts, that was averted.

Pope John had also by this time received his death sentence. Doctors had informed him not long before the council began that he was suffering from terminal cancer, so he knew he did not have much time left in which to try to do something. Almost immediately following the Cuban Missile Crisis he began drafting what would become *Pacem in Terris*. He promulgated it just two months before his death in 1963. It has been appropriately called St. John's "last will and testament," and it is a truly significant document.

For the first time ever, an encyclical is addressed not merely to Catholics but to "all men of goodwill." This is more than mere courtesy: for Pope John, the answer to peace on earth is to be found not just in the relationships between nations and governments but within each human being as a child of God. The encyclical was also destined to have considerable influence on the development of council documents, especially the Declaration on Religious Freedom (*Dignitatis Humanae*) and the Pastoral Constitution on the Church in the Modern World (*Gaudium et Spes*), as the council fathers made the pope's words their own.

*Pacem in Terris* had an influence far beyond the church. In 1965, Robert Hutchens, head of the Center for Democratic Institutions in the United States, described *Pacem in Terris* as "one of the most profound and significant documents of our age . . . which consigns nuclear arms, nationalism, colonialism, racism, and non-constitutional regimes to the wastebasket of history."[11]

Pope John begins the encyclical by describing the "marvelous order" that exists in God's creation. Furthermore, God has created human beings in God's own image and likeness, with intelligence and freedom. How is the order that should be present within each person to be reconciled with the "disunity among individuals and among nations which is in striking contrast to this perfect order in the universe [?] One would think that the relationships that bind [people] together could only be governed by force" (PT 4). The pope concludes that God has placed this order within each person:

> These laws clearly indicate how a man must behave toward his fellows in society, and how the mutual relationships between the members of a State and its officials are to be conducted. They show too

what principles must govern the relations between States; and finally, what should be the relations between individuals or States on the one hand, and the world-wide community of nations on the other. Men's common interests make it imperative that at long last a world-wide community of nations be established. (PT 7)

This global impact is perhaps what makes this encyclical so appropriate for deacons: as ministers of the church's *diakonia* deacons have a special interest not only in assuring the rights of individuals but also how those relationships affect the broader relationships between communities and nations. With deacons serving both in the sanctuary and in the world, it gives us a road map for ministry. Because every human being is a person with intelligence and free will, one therefore has rights and duties that flow from one's human nature. Pope John writes, "These rights and duties are universal and inviolable, and therefore altogether inalienable" (PT 9). This point bears emphasis: The rights of human beings come from their very being—and people of faith would go further to recognize that such rights come from God, and not from any other human agency. Rights are rights, not because they are granted by law (either civil or canon law) or by government fiat, but because they inhere in the very fact of being humans created and graced by God.

### Fundamental Rights

Pope John begins by listing certain fundamental rights all people have: the right to live, the right to bodily integrity and to the means necessary for the proper development of life, particularly food, clothing, shelter, medical care, rest, and necessary social services. He also lists the right to be looked after in the event of ill health, disability stemming from work, widowhood, old age, enforced unemployment, "or whenever through no fault of his own he is deprived of the means of livelihood" (PT 11).

### Rights Pertaining to Moral and Cultural Values

Every person has a right to be respected, to his or her good name, to freedom in investigating the truth, to freedom of speech and publication, to freedom to pursue any profession, and to be accurately informed about public events. Every person has the right to share in the benefits of culture, to receive a good general education, to technical or professional training. Gifted persons have a right to engage in advanced studies.

### The Right to Worship God According to One's Conscience

Every person has the right to worship God in accordance with one's conscience "and to profess his religion both in private and in public" (PT 14).

### "The Right to Choose Freely One's State in Life"

All people have the right to choose their state in life, and the pope speaks of founding a family, in which "both the man and the woman enjoy equal rights and duties," or the priesthood or religious life. The family is the "natural, primary cell of human society" so that families must be considered carefully in social and economic affairs, and within the realm of faith and morals. Within the family the support and education of children is an additional right that belongs primarily to the parents (PT 15–17).

### Economic Rights

Every person has the right for an opportunity to work, and a right to the proper conditions of work (by this the pope is referring to employment practices, and he warns against practices that weaken or harm a person's physical or moral life, or prevent proper human development, such as unfair treatment of adolescents).

A person has a right to engage in economic activity, workers have a right to a just wage, and the pope particularly stresses that right. A worker is entitled to a wage that gives the family a standard of living consistent with human dignity. Everyone has a right to own property.

### The Right of Meeting and Association

Every person has a right to meet and to form associations with other persons, and a right to organize those associations as they wish. The pope writes of the need for intermediate associations designed to assist individuals with matters beyond individual competence.

### The Right to Emigrate and Immigrate

Every person has the right to freedom of movement and residence within one's own country, and also has the right to emigrate to other countries and live there. "The fact that he is a citizen of a particular

State does not deprive him of membership in the human family, nor of citizenship in that universal society, the common, world-wide fellowship of men" (PT 25).

### Political Rights

Every person has the right to be active in public life and contribute to the common good. One has a right to legal protection of one's rights, "and such protection must be effective, unbiased, and strictly just" (PT 27).

### Duties

After listing all of these natural rights, Pope John links them to their parallel obligations; every right is partnered with an obligation. The right to live is matched with an obligation to preserve one's life. The right to educate one's children is matched by the obligation to do so. Likewise, a person's right is matched by a corresponding obligation of others to honor that right. The pope stresses this fact: that rights must always be balanced by the commensurate obligation. "Hence, to claim one's rights and ignore one's duties, or only half fulfill them, is like building a house with one hand and tearing it down with the other. For example, it is useless to admit that a man has a right to the necessities of life, unless we also do all in our power to supply him with means sufficient for his livelihood" (PT 31–32).

## Rights in the Law

Many of these rights expressed by Pope John in *Pacem in Terris* (1963) will twenty years later find their way into the revised Code of Canon Law (1983). It is important to repeat a point made at the beginning of this section: that human rights are from God and that they do not come because any human agency grants them. So, when we speak of rights under the law—in this case, canon law—it is perhaps better to say that the rights mentioned are being supported, defended, and perhaps implemented by the law, not that the law is creating those rights. Finally, a reminder that because of the nature of rights, they apply equally to every human being without exception. Consider the impact of such a claim on the practical aspects of ministry: every human being is entitled to all of these rights, not simply those who are deemed "worthy" of assistance or concern.

The following are some examples of human rights as enshrined in the current Code of Canon Law:

1. The fundamental equality of all Christians based on baptism, and equality and dignity in action; the right and freedom to cooperate in the building up of the Body of Christ (c. 208)
2. The right to evangelize nations (c. 211)
3. The right to petition, that is, to make known to one's superiors (pastors, bishops, and others) one's needs, especially one's spiritual needs, as well as one's hopes (c. 212 §2)
4. The right to make recommendations: the right to advise pastors regarding the good of the church, and the right to participate in the formation of public opinion and in the process of informing the faithful (c. 212 §3)
5. The right to receive the Word of God and the sacraments from one's pastors (c. 213)
6. The right to participate in the public worship of the church in accordance with the legitimate norms of one's own rite (c. 214)
7. The right to one's own proper spirituality (c. 214)
8. The right to association: the right to found and to direct associations that have charitable purposes, and that can be made to exist as an expression of Christian vocation/calling (c. 215)
9. The right to assembly: the right to hold meetings for the same purpose as to associate (c. 215)
10. The right to promote the apostolate and to one's own proper initiative in apostolic work, based on the right to participate in the general mission of the church itself (c. 216)
11. The right to a Christian education (c. 217)
12. Academic freedom: the right to research, and the right to publish (c. 218)
13. Freedom from coercion in choosing one's station in life (c. 218)
14. The right to keep and preserve one's good name and reputation (c. 220)
15. Privacy: the right to have others respect what is most intimate to one's self (c. 220)
16. The right to vindicate one's rights in a court of the church and to defend those rights in the courts of the church (c. 221 §1), with equity, and in accordance with the law (c. 221 §2)
17. The right to be judged (c. 221 §2)

18. The right to the legal process regarding sanctions; that is, the right to expect the church to impose sanctions in accordance with the law (c. 221 §3)

## Conclusions for the Deacon

At this point it is good to recall the very reason ordained ministries exist according to the teaching of the Second Vatican Council:

> In order to ensure that the people of God would have pastors and would enjoy continual growth, Christ the Lord set up in his church a variety of offices [ministries] whose aim is the good of the whole body. Ministers, invested with a sacred power, are at the service of their brothers and sisters, so that all who belong to the people of God and therefore enjoy true Christian dignity may attain to salvation through their free, combined and well-ordered efforts in pursuit of a common goal. (LG 18)

Every time the object of ministry is mentioned, it is communal in nature: "the good of the whole body," "at the service of their brothers and sisters," "all who belong to the people of God," "a common goal." Deacons, empowered by the sacramental grace of ordination, seek the salvation of all: the "spiritual purpose" mentioned by Provost as the highest goal of the church. Deacons work for this goal by working for the dignity of all, the dignity expressed through the rights and commensurate obligations we have reviewed in this chapter.

This pursuit of human dignity is not restricted only to Catholics or to other Christians. As St. John XXIII made clear throughout *Pacem in Terris*, and which the documents of the council will reiterate, human dignity is a universal goal, expressed through the variety of rights from God. Some years ago, during a fund-raising event for the Catholic Charities organization in his archdiocese, the archbishop was asked how many of the people who would receive help would be Catholics. Without a moment's hesitation, the archbishop replied, "We're not doing this because they are Catholics, but because we are."

Deacons, therefore, are ordained to serve everyone in need, without exception. While ordained ministers, including deacons, are most commonly associated with local parishes, the reality must be more universal. Deacons are ordained by the bishop to extend the bishop's reach, to go into places where the presence of the church's ministers has not yet been. As we shall examine in more detail in the next chapter, the question for the deacon should be, "Whose needs in the community are not being met?" These needs are often associated with the inherent rights of people, and the deacon's ministry becomes focused on securing those rights. The Congregation for Clergy, in the Directory for the Ministry and Life of Permanent Deacons, states,

> It must not be forgotten that the object of Christ's *diakonia* is mankind. Every human being carries the traces of sin but is called to communion with God. God so loved the world that He gave His only Son, so that all who believe in Him might not die but have eternal life" (John 3:16). It was for this plan of love that Christ became a slave and took human flesh. The Church continues to be the sign and instrument of that *diakonia* in history. . . . Growth in imitation of Christ's love for mankind—which surpasses all ideologies—is thus an essential component of the spiritual life of every deacon. (DMLPD 49)

We now turn to specific applications of this universal mission of mercy, charity, and justice in the ministry of the deacon.

# CHAPTER 7

# "Moved with Compassion": Deacon at Work as Witness and Guide

## Introduction: The Hands of God's Mercy

Since his election, Pope Francis has been a prophet of God's mercy, and it is this mercy that grounds this chapter and the ministry of the deacon. We take as inspiration the parable of the Good Samaritan (Luke 10:30-37), in which Christ exemplifies his answer about the greatest commandment, love of God, which is tied to love of neighbor:

> "A man was going down from Jerusalem to Jericho, and fell into the hands of robbers, who stripped him, beat him, and went away, leaving him half dead. Now by chance a priest was going down that road; and when he saw him, he passed by on the other side. So likewise a Levite, when he came to the place and saw him, passed by on the other side. But a Samaritan while traveling came near him; and when he saw him, he was moved with pity. He went to him and bandaged his wounds, having poured oil and wine on them. Then he put him on his own animal, brought him to an inn, and took care of him. The next day he took out two denarii, gave them to the innkeeper, and said, 'Take care of him; and when I come back, I will repay you whatever more you spend.' Which of these three, do you think, was a neighbor to the man who fell into the hands of the robbers?" He said, "The one who showed him mercy." Jesus said to him, "Go and do likewise." (Luke 10:30-37)

Even though the lawyer responding to Jesus' question would not even speak the word "Samaritan," he recognized the essential characteristic of neighborliness: mercy. And this mercy flowed from another fact that distinguished the Samaritan from the priest and Levite: when he saw the victim, he was moved with pity. The neighbor in the parable is not the victim, but the Samaritan, responding as a good disciple should. Moved with pity over the suffering of another, the disciple-neighbor responds with mercy.

The word "mercy" is interesting when looking at its Latin roots. The word itself is *misericordia*, and it is made up of two basic elements. *Miseria* is translated as wretchedness, an unhappy condition, misfortune, affliction, distress, misery. *Cor* is, of course, the heart. *Misericordia* then reflects not only a simple act of dispassionate ("without suffering") charity, but rather compassionate ("to suffer with") mercy. Other definitions of *misericordia* capture this connection: "tenderheartedness, compassion, pity." In the gospels, Jesus is often presented as being moved by pity or compassion by those he encounters in misery or suffering from afflictions. Mercy, then, involves the disciple as much as it does the one being helped. This is what marks the difference between a charitable act done by a believer and the same charitable act done by someone who is not.

A medical student once asked me, as part of her research for class, to describe my last visit to the doctor's office and how I felt about the experience. I told her that once I got to see the doctor, everything was fine, but that I had been disappointed earlier in the process. Two assistants had escorted me to the exam room. They immediately went to the computer in the room as I sat down on the exam table. With their backs to me the whole time, they began inputting information about me into the computer. Every so often, one of them would throw a look over her shoulder and ask me a quick question, and then turn back to the computer to make the entry. There was no interpersonal contact at all: everything was about getting my information into the computer without actually relating to me! When they were finished at the computer, they left the room, with one of them telling me as she closed the door that the doctor would be in shortly. I shared with the medical student how impersonal that was, even if they got the data correctly placed into the system. There was no compassion and no sense of mercy.

The church's ministers of mercy, charity, and justice are (because of sacramental initiation) disciples of Christ first and need to be imitators of his own compassionate mercy, not simply the dispensers of a cold, dispassionate charity. Pope Benedict XVI addresses this in *Deus Caritas Est*: "The command of love of neighbor is inscribed by the Creator in the human being's very nature . . . [and] Christianity constantly revives and acts out of this imperative. . . . [I]t is very important that the Church's charitable activity maintains all of its splendor and does not become just another form of social assistance" (31). The pope offers several essential elements that distinguish the church's charitable ministry. Here we will consider only one of them:

> Following the example given in the parable of the Good Samaritan, Christian charity is first of all the simple response to immediate needs and specific situations: feeding the hungry, clothing the naked, caring for and healing the sick, visiting those in prison, etc. . . . Individuals who care for those in need must first be professionally competent: they should be properly trained in what to do and how to do it, and committed to continuing care. Yet, while professional competence is a primary, fundamental requirement, it is not of itself sufficient. We are dealing with human beings, and human beings always need something more than technically proper care. They need humanity. They need heartfelt concern. Those who work for the Church's charitable organizations must be distinguished by the fact that they do not merely meet the needs of the moment, but they dedicate themselves to others with heartfelt concern, enabling them to experience the richness of their humanity. Consequently, in addition to their necessary professional training, these charity workers need a "formation of the heart": they need to be led to that encounter with God in Christ which awakens their love and opens their spirits to others. As a result, love of neighbor will no longer be for them a commandment imposed, so to speak, from without, but a consequence deriving from their faith, a faith which becomes active through love (cf. Gal 5:6). (Ibid.)

With this in mind, we now return to the specific role of the deacon in the ministries of charity as both *witness* and *guide*.[1] I have written previously on several issues in this regard, and I hope that the current text can be read as an addition to the previous work.[2]

## The Deacon as Witness to Charity and Justice

To be a witness to something involves many things. On one level there is the obvious and common understanding of someone who "sees" and "gives testimony" about what has been seen. In this context, the deacon-as-disciple testifies about what he has already received: a loving relationship with the risen Christ. Because of that relationship, the deacon-as-disciple acts upon it: because of Christ's own *kenosis*, the deacon imitates Christ in emptying himself for the common good of others. And it is here that *witness* assumes its more foundational and technical sense. *Witness* translates the Greek *martus* (μάρτυς), *martyr*. The true Christian witness is one who testifies about Christ with his or her very life. "No one has greater love than this," Christ taught about himself, "to lay down one's life for one's friends" (John 15:13). The deacon, then, is a minister who has been called, formed, and sent to proclaim the Good News through a complete self-donation to Christ and to others.

This witness is carried out in many ways. Pope Benedict, in *Deus Caritas Est*, cautions that

> Christian charitable activity must be independent of parties and ideologies. It is not a means of changing the world ideologically, and it is not at the service of worldly stratagems, but it is a way of making present here and now the love which man always needs. We contribute to a better world only by personally doing good now, with full commitment and wherever we have the opportunity, independently of partisan strategies and programs. The Christian's program —the program of the Good Samaritan, the program of Jesus—is "a heart which sees." This heart sees where love is needed and acts accordingly. (31)

Furthermore, Pope Benedict writes, "Love is free; it is not practiced as a way of achieving other ends. . . . Those who practice charity in the Church's name will never seek to impose the Church's faith upon others." He states that the church's charitable structures—and certainly I would specify the church's ordained ministers such as her deacons—should stress this point with others, so that "they may be credible witnesses to Christ" (ibid.).

In short, the deacon—in his own life and example—lives the very *diakonia* he preaches and teaches. The charge to the deacon at ordination, to "believe what you read, teach what you believe, and practice what you teach," is expressed powerfully by the sign of his own actions incarnating the *diakonia* of the church and the mercy of God. The deacon is to be a person of integrity who not only talks the talk but also walks the walk.

## The Deacon as Guide for Charity and Justice

John Paul II, in his 1987 address to the diaconate community gathered in Detroit, summarized two decades of papal teaching on the diaconate:

> The service of the deacon is the Church's service sacramentalized. Yours is not just one ministry among others, but it is truly meant to be, as Paul VI described it, a "driving force" for the Church's *diakonia*. You are meant to be living signs of the servanthood of Christ's Church.[3]

In his 2000 address to deacons and their families in Rome on the occasion of the jubilee day for deacons, St. John Paul II referred to deacons as "active apostles":

> Dear deacons, be active apostles of the new evangelization. Lead everyone to Christ! Through your efforts, may his kingdom also spread in your family, in your workplace, in the parish, in the Diocese, in the whole world![4]

In short, then, deacons are disciples who because of their sacramental ordination are now also apostles with a mission. This relationship between the deacon's discipleship on the one hand and the deacon's apostleship on the other is critical for understanding the deacon's ministerial identity. As disciples, deacons remain connected with Christ; as "active apostles of the New Evangelization," deacons extend themselves and pour themselves out in service to Christ, just as Christ did himself. The deacon's mission is to empty himself (*kenosis*) just as Christ has, even to the point of giving our lives for others in imitation of Christ, our Master.

The Second Vatican Council wrote that "the church encompasses with its love all those who are afflicted by human infirmity and it recognizes in those who are poor and who suffer, the likeness of its poor and suffering founder. It does all in its power to relieve their need and in them it endeavours to serve Christ" (LG 8). The bishops of the United States, building on this teaching, wrote, "Thus, in the communion of life, love, and service realized under the leadership of the successors of the apostles, a vision of reconciled humanity is offered to the world" (National Directory 21). The successors of the apostles, the bishops, have as their assistants the Order of Deacons. This is the nature of the apostolic leadership of the deacon in the exercise of ministry.

## The Venues of the Deacon's Apostolate of Mercy

Where does the deacon exercise his part of the church's mission of mercy, charity, justice, and leadership? When all is said and done, the short answer is, "Wherever there are needs!" The Congregation for Clergy's Directory for the Ministry and Life of Permanent Deacons puts it this way: "Throughout history the service of deacons has taken on various forms so as to satisfy the diverse needs of the Christian community and to enable that community to exercise its mission of charity. It is for the bishops alone, since they rule and have charge of the particular Churches 'as Vicars and legates of Christ,' to confer ecclesiastical office on each deacon according to the norm of law" (DMLPD 40).

Let us consider a number of ways and venues in which deacons may serve. Several of these items have been the subject of prior work, but I hope to develop them further while adding additional considerations. We will begin with the normal venues of diaconal ministry: the parish, the diocese, and regional approaches. This will be a kind of framework for the types of ministry deacons may perform within those venues.

### Official Venues for Ministry: Parish

The parish is the most common assignment for deacons, much like it is for priests. It is here that deacons generally exercise their ministries of Word and Sacrament. In fact, the current stressors on parish life, not the least of which is the ongoing shortage of presbyters in many areas, can create pressure on the deacon to focus on these ministries more than any other. With regard to the church's social justice ministry at the parish level, deacons are often involved when such ministries exist, although in many parishes social justice ministries are generally the responsibility of volunteers who take them on as personal ministries, rather than a conscious, intentional, and universally shared aspect of parish life. Can more be done in this regard? What can the deacon do in leadership of such an effort? Cardinal Walter Kasper has written,

> Each parish has to make sure that *diakonia* is realized. . . . A non-diaconal parish celebrating the Eucharist may express its faith, but

its faith remains dead; in the final analysis it cannot find God, as they miss the point that God reveals himself in the people, especially in the poor.

The Church lives wherever the corporal works of mercy are practiced: feeding the hungry, giving drink to the thirsty, clothing the naked, giving shelter to strangers, liberating prisoners, visiting the sick and burying the dead. The Church also lives wherever the spiritual works of mercy are practiced; correcting sinners, teaching the ignorant, giving counsel to the doubters, comforting the distressed, enduring the troublesome, forgiving those who offend us, praying for the living and the dead.[5]

Pope Francis has picked up on this theme in *Misericordiae Vultus*:

It is my burning desire that, during this Jubilee, the Christian people may reflect on the corporal and spiritual works of mercy. It will be a way to reawaken our conscience, too often grown dull in the face of poverty. . . . Jesus introduces us to these works of mercy in his preaching so that we can know whether or not we are living as his disciples. Let us rediscover these corporal works of mercy. . . . And let us not forget the spiritual works of mercy. . . . We cannot escape the Lord's words to us, and they will serve as the criteria upon which we will be judged. (15)

Deacons could consider the works of mercy as a checklist for parish outreach for charity and justice. Remember the model of the Good Samaritan, who models, among other things, how charity and justice relate. The Samaritan meets the immediate needs of the victim by binding up his wounds and getting him to safety (charity); he also provides for the victim in a more long-term way as well (justice). If a person is hungry, we feed him or her; that's charity. Working to eliminate the causes of hunger in the first place is to seek after justice. The deacon could associate himself with other leaders in the parish to coordinate both charitable and justice-related responses through the corporal and spiritual works of mercy. It should also be noted that these efforts should not be limited, of course, to serving the members of the parish. The response to all of these needs could extend far beyond the boundaries of the parish, although the first venue of leadership in these issues is—or ought to be—the parish. As efforts expand, the deacons in neighboring parishes could form a leadership team that extends the efforts even further.

The Congregation for the Clergy provides some additional canonical insight to the deacon's ministry in parish-based ministry. "The bishop may give deacons the task of cooperating with a parish priest in the parish (c. 519) entrusted to him or in the pastoral care of several parishes entrusted *in solidum* to one or more priests (c. 517 §1)" (DMLPD 41). In the case of deacons assigned to parishes that do not have an assigned pastor (c. 517 §2), "they always have precedence over the non-ordained faithful" (ibid.).

Deacons may also be called to guide dispersed Christian communities in the name of the bishop or the parish priest.[6] "This is a missionary function to be carried out in those territories, environments, social strata and groups where priests are lacking or cannot be easily found. In particular, in those areas where no priest is available to celebrate the Eucharist, the deacon brings together and guides the community in a celebration of the word with the distribution of Holy Communion which has been duly reserved."[7] When deacons supply in places where there is a shortage of priests, they do so by ecclesial mandate."[8] Deacons are also members of parish pastoral councils by right.[9]

### Official Venues for Ministry: Regional-Diocesan Ministry

Like priests, deacons are incardinated as ministers in service to the entire diocese. Unfortunately, too often deacons are perceived as parish-based ministers only. The central finding of a 1996 study by the United States Catholic Conference (now the United States Conference of Catholic Bishops) contains some interesting points:

> The restored Order of the Diaconate, largely parish-based, has been successful and increasingly important for the life of the Church. *The primary challenges of the diaconate for the future are to broaden its ministries beyond its largely successful and increasingly indispensable adaptation to parish life* and *to emphasize more strongly that deacons, through ordination, are called to be model, animator, and facilitator of ministries of charity and justice within the local church.*[10]

Already twenty years ago, the bishops were calling for an expanded scope to the deacon's ministry. While some dioceses have implemented policies in which bishops are giving deacons a dual assignment: one to a parish, usually for the exercise of the ministries of Word and Sacrament, and a second to another institutional or diocesan ministry for the exercise of a ministry of charity and justice. Much more can be done.

For example, most deacons receive their assignments as individuals. What if groups of deacons could take on particular ministries together? Based on shared interests, regional needs, a fraternity of deacons could multiply their effectiveness in ways that could far exceed their individual efforts.

Once again, consider the Directory for the Ministry and Life of Permanent Deacons: "Numerous opportunities for the fruitful exercise of the ministry of deacons arise at diocesan level. Indeed, when they possess the necessary requirements, deacons may act as members of diocesan bodies, in particular diocesan pastoral councils[11] and diocesan finance councils, and take part in diocesan synods (c. 463 §2)" (DMLPD 42). Deacons may not be members of the presbyteral council since the law restricts that role to the presbyterate.

If the deacon holds the necessary qualifications, he may serve as diocesan chancellor (c. 482), judge (c. 1421 §1), assessor (c. 1424), auditor (c. 1428 §2), promoter of justice and defender of the bond (c. 1435), and notary (c. 483 §1). Deacons may not serve as judicial vicars, adjunct judicial vicars, or vicars forane; these offices are reserved for priests.

> Other areas in which deacons may exercise their ministry include diocesan commissions, pastoral work in specific social contexts—especially the pastoral care of the family—or among particular groups with special pastoral needs, such as ethnic minorities.
>
> In the exercise of the above offices, the deacon should recall that every action in the Church should be informed by charity and service to all. In judicial, administrative and organizational matters, deacons should always strive to avoid unnecessary forms of bureaucracy, lest they deprive their ministry of pastoral meaning and value. Those deacons who are called to exercise such offices should be placed so as to discharge duties which are proper to the diaconate, in order to preserve the integrity of the diaconal ministry. (DMLPD 42)

### *Official Venues for Ministry: Community-Based Ministry*

We have already referenced St. John Paul II's famous quotation about the renewed diaconate: "A deeply felt need in the decision to re-establish the permanent diaconate was and is that of greater and more direct presence of Church ministers in the various spheres of the family, work, school, etc., in addition to existing pastoral structures."[12] Here is where particular creativity is necessary. The question would be, What needs, whose needs, are not currently being met? Deacons, after all, have traditionally been seen as the eyes and ears of the bishop in identifying and meeting needs. Are the deacons of a diocese encouraged to be creative in their ministry? Deacons can and should exercise leadership in community-based service initiatives. Conformed in a special way to Christ "the Head and Servant" (in the words of St. John Paul II), the deacon imitates Christ in reaching out beyond the limits of the church. This is an area requiring much more development in the future.

## Reprise: The Deacon and *Gaudium et Spes*

Some years ago, Msgr. Paul McPartlan drew a connection between the deacon and the capstone document of the Second Vatican Council, the Pastoral Constitution on the Church in the Modern World (*Gaudium et Spes*).[13] A few years later, I included a brief reflection on the same connection, focusing on "urgent moral questions" raised by the council fathers as they might apply to the ministry of the deacon.[14] I continue to maintain that the deacon's involvement in ministries of mercy, charity, and justice can still find resonance, inspiration, and an agenda for ministerial action in those issues. Therefore, I want to revisit these crucial issues, which remain no less urgent today than they were fifty years ago when they were promulgated by the council.

Part 2 of *Gaudium et Spes*, which contains these urgent issues, was drafted as an appendix to the main document, but the council fathers decided instead that the issues being highlighted were of such critical importance that they should not be relegated to an appendix, but were part of the very fabric of the Constitution itself.

> Of the many problems which are matters of universal concern nowadays, it may be helpful to concentrate on the following: marriage and the family, culture, economic and social life, politics, the solidarity of peoples, and peace. We must seek light for each of these problems from the principles which Christ has given us; in this way the faithful will receive guidance and all people will be enlightened in their search for solutions to so many complex problems. (GS 46)

As we pointed out in our discussion of *Pacem in Terris*, there was a prevalent attitude shared by St. John XXIII and most of the bishops that the problems of the world were not simply Catholic issues, but universal concerns. This means that the solutions would require all people to be involved. Notice the citation above: all people are to be enlightened, and all people need to search for solutions to these problems. Deacons, as ordained ministers, have a leadership responsibility for assisting in this discernment and coordinating appropriate responses.

### Marriage and the Family

Pope Francis has taken concrete steps, by means of the synodal process, to address the many questions affecting marriage and family life. Certainly deacons are in a particularly strong position to witness to the beauty and grace-filled nature of marriage and the family. They can also guide others on their own journey. What are the initiatives going on already in your parish, local community, or diocese that the deacon may already be involved with? What other ways might be set up to do a better job? Families today are under terrific stress; deacons can be wonderful leaders of efforts to offer more substantive support.

How might creative responses be sought? Might this be a good area for several deacons to come together and provide regional support?

### Proper Development of Culture

It's a constant refrain from many: that today's culture is in decline and that we need to do all we can to reverse it. There is no argument that we ourselves control our own culture, but what specifically can be done about it? Consider the words of the bishops: "In each nation and social group there is a growing number of men and women who are conscious that they themselves are the architects and molders of their community's culture" (GS 55).

The church is to be the leaven and soul of society, and her deacons should be deeply involved in how that gets done. The 1998 Directory for the Ministry and Life of Permanent Deacons recalls *Gaudium et Spes*: "The deacon should be conversant with contemporary cultures and with the aspirations and problems of his times. . . . In this context, indeed, he is called to be a living sign of Christ the Servant and to assume the Church's responsibility of 'reading the signs of the time and of interpreting them in the light of the Gospel'" (DMLPD 43).

Again we turn to the personal: is the proper development of culture something that marks me as a human being? Do I demonstrate in my own life respect for others through my choice of language, by my acts of respect for others, by my own refusal to be drawn into behaviors and attitudes which demean, cheapen or ridicule others? This is where the transformation of culture begins. Does this extend outward into our family life, and into the parish and broader community? Are there efforts being undertaken at parish and community levels with which I can become associated? If not, might I be able to start something?[15]

### Economic and Social Life

The Second Vatican Council teaches,

> In the sphere of economic and social life, too, the dignity and vocation of the human person as well as the welfare of society as a whole have to be respected and fostered; for people are the source, the focus and the aim of all economic and social life. (GS 63)

Since the council the economic disparities between rich and poor have only gotten worse. "Luxury and misery exist side by side" (ibid.). Here again, the deacon can be the minister of the church who takes the lead in finding local resources to help in charity, but also to find ways to reform inequitable economic policies where they exist. Is there, perhaps even with the local diaconate community, economic and financial expertise that can be put to work? "It's important to perform the corporal works of mercy: to feed the hungry, to clothe the naked, to shelter the homeless and so on; but what are the conditions that led to their hunger, their nakedness and their homelessness? The servant Christian quietly finds ways, not only to offer immediate help and support, but ways to begin addressing the social, political and economic causes of the need."[16]

> Christians engaged actively in modern economic and social progress and in the struggle for justice and charity must be convinced that they have much to contribute to the prosperity of humanity and to world peace. Let them, as individuals and as a group, give a shining example to others. (GS 72)

### The Political Community

The increasing polarization in politics, especially here in the United States, is also considerably worse today than it was fifty years ago. But the words they wrote then might have been written just this morning:

> In our times profound transformations are to be noticed in the structure and institutions of nations; they are the accompaniment of

cultural, economic, and social development. These transformations exercise a deep influence on political life, particularly as regards the rights and duties of the individual, in the exercise of civil liberty and in the achievement of the common good." (GS 73)

This question has particular relevance for deacons, since canon law does not prevent (permanent) deacons from taking an active role in political life (all other clerics are forbidden to do so). Particular law in the United States requires that deacons get written permission from the bishops before entering into public political life, but many deacons have received such permission and are quite involved in politics. Because of this unique opportunity for deacons to serve, it is important to reflect on the issues involved.

This topic becomes even more complicated since increasingly deacons are joining millions of other Americans in their use of social media and are blogging, tweeting, writing, speaking, and teaching at every conceivable level, and even venues formerly considered more informal, such as Facebook, have become sources of public discourse on the political process. It is important to reflect on the deacon's participation in such exchanges in light of our responsibilities as clergy. In today's technical world, it can be that what a deacon says from the pulpit can be overshadowed quickly by a casual "status update" on Facebook, a blog entry, or a tweet.

Canon 285 directs, "Clerics are to refrain completely from all those things which are unbecoming to their state, according to the prescripts of particular law" (§1). The canon continues in §3: "Clerics are forbidden to assume public offices which entail a participation in the exercise of civil power," and §4 forbids clerics from "secular offices which entail an obligation of rendering accounts. . . ." Canon 287 §1 reminds all clerics, "Most especially, [they] are always to foster the peace and harmony based on justice which are to be observed among people," and §2 directs, "They are not to have an active part in political parties and in governing labor unions unless, in the judgment of competent ecclesiastical authority, the protection of the rights of the Church or the promotion of the common good requires it."

However, c. 288 specifically relieves permanent deacons (transitional deacons would still be bound) of a number of the prior canons, including cc. 285 §§3 and 4 and 287 §2, "unless particular law establishes otherwise." Particular law in this instance is provided by the National

Directory for the Formation, Ministry, and Life of Permanent Deacons in the United States, which states: "A permanent deacon may not present his name for election to any public office or in any other general election, or accept a nomination or an appointment to public office, without the prior written permission of the diocesan bishop. A permanent deacon may not actively and publicly participate in another's political campaign without the prior written permission of the diocesan bishop" (91). The diocesan bishop may also create particular law within his own diocese on such matters. In one case, a diocesan bishop notified his clergy that if anyone could even infer, through their speech, manner, or demeanor, which political party or candidate the cleric was supporting, then that cleric had gone too far. While deacons are each entitled to form their own political decisions, they must always be aware of the political lines they must not cross.

I have been asked if this means that deacons are not permitted to put campaign yard signs or posters on their property, or political bumper stickers on their cars. It would be my opinion that, based on universal and particular law, the deacon should not do so. Such public displays, again in my opinion, would violate both the letter and intent of the law. What about making financial contributions to a particular campaign or political party? I believe that this all becomes an issue of public and private participation, but in all cases, I would seek advice from competent authority on the diocesan staff or from the bishop directly.

To sum up: Permanent deacons, although clerics, may participate in political life to a degree not permitted other clerics (including transitional deacons) under the law. However, permanent deacons are required by particular law in the United States to obtain the prior written permission of their diocesan bishop to do so. I find that two other aspects of this matter are too often overlooked. First is the requirement under the law that all clerics (and, most significantly, permanent deacons are *not* relieved of this obligation) are bound by c. 287 always "to foster peace and harmony based on justice." This is such a critical point for reflection for all clerics: How do our actions, words, and insinuations foster such peace and harmony, or are our actions serving to sow discord and disharmony? Since permanent deacons may become more engaged in the political sphere than presbyters (with the permission of their bishop), this will take on particular relevance for deacons. Second is the whole area of participation in political campaigns. Deacons may only participate in their own *or someone else's* political campaign with the prior written permission of their bishop. Today, when political support is often reflected through social media, all of us might well reflect on how our opinions stated via these media constitute active participation in someone's political campaign.

There is a fine moral and legal tightrope here. On the one hand, it would be wonderful if more deacons—with the permission of their bishops, of course—would enter political life. There are many forms of public life, elected leaders such as mayors and governors but also school boards, judges, and magistrates. A Catholic deacon could make interesting contributions to public discourse. On the other hand, the deacon must also recognize the limitations he is under even if he is not himself in political life. Deacons must constantly remember that they are preaching principles but not political parties.

### Fostering of Peace and the Establishment of a Community of Nations

The last of the urgent needs mentioned by the council fathers is no surprise. Although written after two World Wars and at the height of the Cold War, its message today is no less urgent. The teaching can be summed up well in this brief passage:

> The council proposes to set down the true and noble nature of peace, to condemn the savagery of war, and to encourage Christians to cooperate with all in securing a peace based on justice and charity and in promoting the means necessary to attain it, under the help of Christ, author of peace. (GS 77)

In their discussions, the bishops found particular insights from St. John XXIII's encyclical *Pacem in Terris*, which we have already examined earlier. The bishops were particularly influenced by the late pope's emphasis on the fact that securing the rights of persons is the first step to a true and just peace in the world. The bishops were also influenced greatly by Pope Paul VI's speech to the UN General Assembly in 1964, where he passionately begged the assembled representatives to lay down arms and to never again seek solutions through war and violence.

We have already seen how the deacon can help with working toward securing human rights for all. In addition, this section also challenges us in situations other than traditional warfare. What kind of violence exists already in local neighborhoods and communities? Again, it could be the deacons who take the lead in trying to address the causes of that violence. "True peace is achievable only through seeking the right ordering of biblical justice, and each of us can serve to 'order' things in our immediate vicinities as much as we can."[17]

## Conclusions

The potential ministries of mercy, charity, justice, and leadership available to deacons are unlimited. If "all politics is local," so too are these ministries. That is why we have focused our attention on offering a number of foundation stones upon which such ministries might be constructed.

Central to the whole project has been the notion that ordination conveys a leadership responsibility to the ordinand, along with the sacramental grace necessary to exercise that leadership. Every so often, it might seem that some people perceive the deacon as being ordained to perform acts of charity so that other disciples do not have to do so. As we have seen, however, discipleship carries that obligation, the discipleship initiated through baptism, confirmation, and Eucharist. Ordination adds an additional obligation, the obligation of apostolic servant-leadership. It is crucial that deacon candidates and deacons continue to identify their own leadership styles and strengths. Through ordination, the deacon is a public ecclesial person who now acts in the person of Christ and in the name of the whole church.

In addition, we have reviewed canon law and magisterial texts to suggest the many "supports" that already exist to enable and empower the ministries of the deacon. It is useful to know what can and cannot be done, or even to find areas of leadership available to the deacon that may have been unknown to him before!

Finally, we recall the words of Pope Benedict. In all the deacon's efforts, we must recall the lesson of the Good Samaritan, namely, to be "moved with pity" for those whom we serve. "Practical activity will always be insufficient, unless it visibly expresses a love for man, a love nourished by an encounter with Christ. My deep personal sharing in the needs and sufferings of others becomes a sharing of my very self with them: if my gift is not to prove a source of humiliation, I must give to others not only something that is my own, but my very self; I must be personally present in my gift" (*Deus Caritas Est* 34).

This book is being published at the very beginning of the Jubilee Year of Mercy. Once again, Pope Francis is modeling for us the fundamental truth of God's action in all of our lives: God is merciful to us, and we extend that mercy to others. In a very real sense, deacons serve as the "signs and instruments" of that mercy: the hands of God's mercy.

*"Love is free!"*

# Notes

## Introduction

1. *Lumen Gentium* (LG) 29. The English translation on the Vatican web site has "the diaconate"; in either case, as will be addressed below, "diaconate" is presented as a singular reality.

2. Paul VI, *Hodie concilium*, *Acta Apostolicae Sedis (AAS)* 58 (1966): 57–64.

3. Ignatius, *Trallians* 3:1, in *Early Christian Fathers*, ed. Cyril C. Richardson (New York: Macmillan, 1970), 99.

4. Ignatius, *Magnesians* 6:1, in Richardson, 95.

5. Polycarp, *The Letter of Polycarp to the Philippians* 5:2, in Richardson, 133.

6. See B. Steimer, "*Didascalia*," in *Dictionary of Early Christian Literature*, ed. Siegmar Döpp and Wilhelm Geerlings (New York: Herder & Herder, 2000), 171–72.

7. R. Hugh Connolly, *Didascalia Apostolorum: The Syriac Version* (Oxford: Clarendon Press, 1929), 109.

8. Ibid., 88, 150.

9. Austin Flannery, ed., *Vatican Council II: Constitutions, Decrees, Declarations; The Basic Sixteen Documents* (Collegeville, MN: Liturgical Press, 2014).

10. United States Conference of Catholic Bishops, National Directory for the Formation, Ministry, and Life of Permanent Deacons in the United States (Washington, DC: USCCB, 2005), 39, citing its predecessor document, Bishops' Committee on the Permanent Diaconate, National Conference of Catholic Bishops, Permanent Deacons in the United States: Guidelines on Their Formation and Ministry, 1984 Revision (Washington, DC: United States Catholic Conference, 1985), 43.

11. William T. Ditewig, *The Emerging Diaconate: Servant Leaders in a Servant Church* (Mahwah, NJ: Paulist Press, 2007), 137, citing LG 1 and *Gaudium et Spes* 40.

12. Alister E. McGrath, *Christian Theology: An Introduction*, 4th ed. (Malden, MA: Blackwell, 2007), 251.

13. Paul VI, *Hodie concilium*, *AAS* 58 (1966): 57–64.

14. John Paul II, Allocution to the Permanent Deacons and their Wives Given at Detroit, MI (19 September 1987), *Origins* 17 (1987): 327–29.

## Chapter 1

1. Paul VI, *Hodie concilium*, AAS 58 (1966): 57–64.

2. See William T. Ditewig, *The Emerging Diaconate: Servant Leaders in a Servant Church* (Mahwah, NJ: Paulist Press, 2007).

3. Francis, *Misericordiae Vultus*: Bull of Indiction of the Extraordinary Jubilee of Mercy, April 11, 2015.

4. See, for example, Giuseppe Alberigo and Joseph A. Komonchak, eds., *History of Vatican II*, 5 vols. (Maryknoll, NY: Orbis; Leuven, BE: Peeters, 1995–2006; John W. O'Malley, *What Happened at Vatican II?* (Cambridge, MA: Harvard University Press, 2010).

5. See, for example, Bernard Cooke, *Ministry to Word and Sacraments* (Philadelphia: Fortress, 1976); Kenan B. Osborne, *Priesthood: A History of the Ordained Ministry in the Roman Catholic Church* (New York: Paulist Press, 1988); Kenan B. Osborne, *The Diaconate in the Christian Church* (Chicago: National Association of Diaconate Directors, 1996); William T. Ditewig, *The Emerging Diaconate: Servant Leaders in a Servant Church* (Mahwah, NJ: Paulist Press, 2007); Nathan Mitchell, *Mission and Ministry: History and Theology in the Sacrament of Order* (Wilmington, DE: Michael Glazier, 1982); James M. Barnett, *The Diaconate: A Full and Equal Order*, rev. ed. (Valley Forge, PA: Trinity Press International, 1995); Joseph W. Pokusa, "A Canonical-Historical Study of the Diaconate in the Western Church" (JCD diss., Catholic University of America, 1979); Kenan B. Osborne, *The Permanent Diaconate: Its History and Place in the Sacrament of Orders* (Mahwah, NJ: Paulist Press, 2007).

6. Joseph A. Komonchak, "Who Are the Church?," The Père Marquette Lecture (Milwaukee, WI: Marquette University Press, 2008), 10–11.

7. See B. Steimer, "*Didascalia*," in *Dictionary of Early Christian Literature*, ed. Siegmar Döpp and Wilhelm Geerlings (New York: Herder & Herder, 2000), 171–72.

8. R. Hugh Connolly, *Didascalia Apostolorum: The Syriac Version* (Oxford: Clarendon Press, 1929), 109.

9. Congregation for the Clergy, Directory for the Ministry and Life of Permanent Deacons (Vatican City: Libreria Editrice Vaticana, 1998) (hereafter cited as DMLPD) 9.

## Chapter 2

1. *Catechism of the Catholic Church*, 2nd ed. (United States Catholic Conference—Libreria Editrice Vaticana, 1997) 1691–92, 1694.

2. Rick Hilgartner, "*Lex Orandi, Lex Credendi*: The Word of God in the Celebration of the Sacraments," Resources for Catechetical Sunday 2009 (Washington, DC: USCCB, 2009), 4.

3. Russell B. Connors, *Christian Morality: In the Breath of God* (Chicago: Loyola Press, 2002), 2.

4. Ibid., 5.

## Chapter 3

1. See, for example, Matilda Webb, *The Churches and Catacombs of Early Christian Rome: A Comprehensive Guide* (East Sussex, UK: Sussex Academic Press, 2001); and Thomas F. X. Noble, *The Republic of St. Peter: The Birth of the Papal State, 680-825* (Philadelphia: University of Pennsylvania Press, 1984).

2. John Paul II, catechesis at the General Audience of October 6, 1993, Deacons Serve the Kingdom of God, no. 6, in *Insegnamenti* XVI, 2 (1993): 954.

3. John XXIII, "Allocution for the Opening of the Second Vatican Council," *AAS* 54 (1962): n. 14, 786–96.

4. Paul VI, Address to the Cardinals and the Consultants of the Council for the Code Revision of Canon Law, November 20, 1965: "Nunc admodum mutatis rerum condicionibus . . . ius canonicum, prudentia adhibita, est recognoscendum: scilicet accommodari debet novo mentis habitui, Concilii Oecumenici Vaticani Secundi proprio, ex quo curae pastorali plurimum tribuitur, et novis necessitatibus populi Dei" (*AAS* 57 [1965]: 998).

5. Francis, Apostolic Exhortation *Evangelii Gaudium* (November 24, 2013), 26–27.

6. Ladislas Orsy, "The Meaning of *Novus Habitus Mentis*: The Search for New Horizons," *The Jurist* 48 (1988): 429–47, 429.

7. Ibid., 431.

8. Nathan Mitchell, OSB, *Mission and Ministry: History and Theology in the Sacrament of Order* (Wilmington, DE: Michael Glazier, 1982), 304.

## Chapter 4

1. See Nathan Mitchell, OSB, *Mission and Ministry: History and Theology in the Sacrament of Order* (Wilmington, DE: Michael Glazier, 1982).

2. Announcement of the Jubilee, http://www.im.va/content/gdm/en.html.

3. John P. Beal, "The Exercise of the Power of Governance by Lay People: State of the Question," *The Jurist* 55 (1995): 15.

4. William T. Ditewig, "The Exercise of Governance by Deacons: A Theological and Canonical Study," PhD dissertation (Washington, DC: Catholic University of America, 2003).

5. James H. Provost, "Ecclesiastical Offices," in *New Commentary on the Code of Canon Law*, ed. John P. Beal, James A. Coriden, and Thomas J. Green (New York/ Mahwah, NJ: Paulist Press, 2000), 207.

6. Ibid.

7. Paul VI, *motu proprio Sacrum Diaconatus Ordinem*, June 18, 1967, *AAS* 59 (1967): 697–704.

8. Bertram F. Griffin, "The Three-Fold *Munera* of Christ and the Church," in *Code, Community, Ministry: Selected Studies for the Parish Minister Introducing the Revised Code of Canon Law*, ed. James H. Provost (Washington, DC: Canon Law Society of America, 1982, 1983), 19–20.

9. Ibid., 20.

10. Ibid., 20. See also J. James Cuneo, "The Power of Jurisdiction: Empowerment for Church Functioning and Mission Distinct from the Power of Orders," *The Jurist* 39 (1979): 200: "*Potestas iurisdictionis* would not simply mean ruling function. Rather it too would apply to any of the three types of sacred functions [teaching, sanctifying, ruling] in the Church. It also signifies a means to fulfill these types of functions."

11. See John J. McCarthy, "The *Diakonia* of Charity in the Permanent Diaconate: Its Application to Certain Clerical Offices as Addressed in the *Directory for the Ministry and Life of Permanent Deacons*" (JCD diss., Pontifical University of St. Thomas, Rome, 2000), 107–20.

12. *Communicationes* 13 (1981): 306.

13. McCarthy, "The *Diakonia* of Charity," 114.

14. Ibid.

15. Ibid., 118.

16. Congregation for the Clergy, et al., instruction *Ecclesiae de Mysterio*, August 15, 1997, *AAS* 89 (1997): 852–76; English translation in *Origins* 27 (November 27, 1997): 397–409.

17. Ibid., art. 4.

### Part II: The Mission of Mercy

1. Francis, *Misericordiae Vultus* 1.

2. Ibid. 11, citing John Paul II, *Dives in Misericordia* 13.

3. Herbert Vorgrimler, *Sacramental Theology*, trans. Linda M. Maloney (Collegeville, MN: Liturgical Press, 1992), 270.

4. Ibid.

### Chapter 5

1. John Paul II, Deacons Are Configured to Christ the Servant, November 30, 1995, no. 4.

### Chapter 6

1. James H. Provost, "Canonical Reflection on Selected Issues in Diocesan Governance," in *The Ministry of Governance*, ed. James K. Mallett (Washington, DC: Canon Law Society of America, 1986), 215–16.

2. Ibid., 248–51.

3. Walter Kasper, "The Diaconate," in *Leadership in the Church: How Traditional Roles Can Serve the Christian Community Today* (New York: Crossroad,

2003), 37. Originally published as "Der Diakon in ekklesiologisher Sicht angesichts der gegenwärtigen Herausforderungen in Kirche und Gesellschaft," in *Diakonia* 32/3–4 (1997): 13–33; also in W. Kasper, *Theologie und Kirche* (Mainz: Matthias-Grünewald, 1999), 2:145–62; and as "The Ministry of the Deacon: The Deacon Offers an Ecclesiological View of Current Challenges in the Church and Society," *Deacon Digest* (March/April 1998): 20.

4. Kasper, "The Diaconate," 39.

5. Provost, "Diocesan Governance," 249.

6. Agnes Cunningham, "Power and Authority in the Church," in *The Ministry of Governance*, ed. James K. Mallett (Washington, DC: CLSA, 1986), 80.

7. Karl Rahner, s.v. "Power," in *Sacramentum Mundi: An Encyclopedia of Theology*, ed. Karl Rahner, et al. (New York: Herder and Herder, 1970), 70.

8. James A. Coriden, *Canon Law as Ministry: Freedom and Good Order for the Church* (New York: Paulist Press, 2000), 107.

9. Ibid., 112.

10. Provost, "Diocesan Governance," 249.

11. Edward Reed, ed., *Peace on Earth: Pacem in Terris: The Proceedings of an International Convocation on the Requirements of Peace*, sponsored by the Center for the Study of Democratic Institutions (New York: Pocket Books, 1965), 1.

## Chapter 7

1. The terms "witness" and "guide" are drawn from a section heading in United States Conference of Catholic Bishops, National Directory for the Formation, Ministry, and Life of Permanent Deacons in the United States (Washington, DC: USCCB, 2005).

2. See, for example, William T. Ditewig, *The Emerging Diaconate: Servant Leaders in a Servant Church* (Mahwah, NJ: Paulist Press, 2007); and William T. Ditewig, "The Kenotic Leadership of Deacons," in *The Deacon Reader*, ed. James Keating (Mahwah, NJ: Paulist Press, 2006).

3. John Paul II, Allocution to the Permanent Deacons and their Wives Given at Detroit, MI, September 19, 1987, *Origins* 17 (1987): 327–29.

4. John Paul II, Deacons: Apostles of the New Evangelization, February 19, 2000, no. 2.

5. Walter Kasper, "The Diaconate," in *Leadership in the Church: How Traditional Roles Can Serve the Christian Community Today* (New York: Crossroad, 2003), 23.

6. Cf. Paul VI, *Sacrum Diaconatus Ordinem*, V, 22, 10; *l.c.*, 702.

7. Cf. *CIC*, c. 1248 §2; Congregation for Divine Worship, Directory for celebrations in the absence of the priest, *Christi Ecclesia*, 29, *l.c.*, 386.

8. John Paul II, Catechesis at the General Audience of 13 October 1993, n. 4: *Insegnamenti* XVI, 2 (1993): 1002.

9. Cf. Paul VI, Apostolic Letter *Sacrum Diaconatus Ordinem*, V, 24; *l.c.*, 702; *CIC*, c. 536.

10. United States Catholic Conference, A National Study on the Permanent Diaconate of the Catholic Church in the United States, 1994–1995 (Washington, DC: USCC, 1996), 13, emphasis added.

11. Cf. Paul VI, Apostolic Letter *Sacrum Diaconatus Ordinem*, V, 24; *l.c.*, 702; *CIC*, c. 512 §1.

12. John Paul II, catechesis at the General Audience of October 6, 1993, Deacons Serve the Kingdom of God, no. 6, *Insegnamenti* XVI, 2 (1993): 954.

13. Paul McPartlan, "The Permanent Diaconate and *Gaudium et Spes*," *Briefing* 32, no. 4 (April 2002): 3–10.

14. William T. Ditewig, *The Emerging Diaconate: Servant Leaders in a Servant Church* (Mahwah, NJ: Paulist Press, 2007), 199–206.

15. Ibid., 201–2.

16. Ibid., 202.

17. Ibid., 206.